I0813858

WORLD HISTORY

# AND THE RISE OF GLOBAL CONFLICT

**By Elizabeth Morgan**

Portions of this book originally appeared in *World War I* by Robert Green.

Published in 2017 by
Lucent Press, an Imprint of Greenhaven Publishing, LLC
353 3rd Avenue
Suite 255
New York, NY 10010



Designer: Andrea Davison-Bartolotta & Deanna Paternostro
Editor: Katie Kawa

**Library of Congress Cataloging-in-Publication Data**

Names: Morgan, Elizabeth.
Title: World War I and the rise of global conflict / Elizabeth Morgan.
Description: New York : Lucent Press, 2017. | Series: World history | Includes index.
Identifiers: ISBN 9781534560581 (library bound) | ISBN 9781534560536 (ebook)
Subjects: LCSH: World War, 1914-1918–Juvenile literature.
Classification: LCC D522.7 M67 2017 | DDC 940.4–dc23

Printed in the United States of America

CPSIA compliance information: Batch #CW17KL: For further information contact Greenhaven Publishing LLC, New York, New York at 1-844-317-7404.

Please visit our website, www.greenhavenpublishing.com. For a free color catalog of all our high-quality books, call toll free 1-844-317-7404 or fax 1-844-317-7405.

# CONTENTS


**Foreword** 4
**Setting the Scene: A Timeline** 6

**Introduction:**
*A Nagging Question* 8

**Chapter One:**
*War on the Western Front* 12

**Chapter Two:**
*Fighting at Sea and in the Sky* 27

**Chapter Three:**
*New Battlefronts* 39

**Chapter Four:**
*The Eastern Front* 54

**Chapter Five:**
*America Joins the Fight* 66

**Epilogue:**
*"A Peace to End Peace"* 79

**Notes** 91
**For More Information** 94
**Index** 96
**Picture Credits** 103
**About the Author** 104

# Foreword

History books are often filled with names and dates—words and numbers for students to memorize for a test and forget once they move on to another class. However, what history books should be filled with are great stories, because the history of our world is filled with great stories. Love, death, violence, heroism, and betrayal are not just themes found in novels and movie scripts. They are often the driving forces behind major historical events.

When told in a compelling way, fact is often far more interesting—and sometimes far more unbelievable—than fiction. World history is filled with more drama than the best television shows, and all of it really happened. As readers discover the incredible truth behind the triumphs and tragedies that have impacted the world since ancient times, they also come to understand that everything is connected. Historical events do not exist in a vacuum. The stories that shaped world history continue to shape the present and will undoubtedly shape the future.

The titles in this series aim to provide readers with a comprehensive understanding of pivotal events in world history. They are written with a focus on providing readers with multiple perspectives to help them develop an appreciation for the complexity of the study of history. There is no set lens through which history must be viewed, and these titles encourage readers to analyze different viewpoints to understand why a historical figure acted the way they did or why a contemporary scholar wrote what they did about a historical event. In this way, readers are able to sharpen their critical-thinking skills and apply those skills in their history classes. Readers are aided in this pursuit by formally documented quotations and annotated bibliographies, which encourage further research and debate.

Many of these quotations come from carefully selected primary sources, including diaries, public records, and contemporary research and writings. These valuable primary sources help readers hear the voices of those who directly experienced historical events, as well as the voices of biographers and historians who provide a unique perspective on familiar topics. Their voices all help history come alive in a vibrant way.

As students read the titles in this series, they are provided with clear context in the form of maps, timelines, and informative text. These elements give them the basic facts they need to fully appreciate the high drama that is history.

The study of history is difficult at times—not because of all the information that needs to be memorized, but because of the challenging questions it asks us. How could something as horrible as the Holocaust happen? Why would religious leaders use torture during the Inquisition? Why does ISIS have so many followers? The information presented in each title gives readers the tools they need to confront these questions and participate in the debates they inspire.

As we pore over the stories of events and eras that changed the world, we come to understand a simple truth: No one can escape being a part of history. We are not bystanders; we are active participants in the stories that are being created now and will be written about in history books decades and even centuries from now. The titles in this series help readers gain a deeper appreciation for history and a stronger understanding of the connection between the stories of the past and the stories they are part of right now.

# SETTING THE SCENE: A TIMELINE

**1914**

World War I begins; the Panama Canal opens, shortening sea travel between the Atlantic and the Pacific.

**1915**

Alexander Graham Bell, inventor of the telephone, makes the first transcontinental phone call between New York and San Francisco; U.S. occupation of Haiti begins.

**1916**

John J. Pershing leads U.S. troops into Mexico to search for the revolutionary leader Pancho Villa; during the Easter Rebellion in Ireland, Irish nationalists try to overthrow British rule.

1917

The United States abandons neutrality and joins the Allied Powers fighting in World War I; the czars, or rulers, of Russia are overthrown in the Russian Revolution; suffragettes march on the White House to protest the fact that American women cannot vote.

1918

Armistice is signed between Allied and Central Powers, ending the fighting of World War I; an outbreak of Spanish influenza kills millions of people; daylight saving time is officially adopted in the United States.

1919

The Treaty of Versailles is signed, formally ending World War I; the British army guns down unarmed civilians in the town of Amritsar, India, leading for more calls for the end of British rule in India.

INTRODUCTION

# A NAGGING QUESTION

World War I was once called the "war to end all wars." However, it ultimately did not live up to that promise. Instead, it gave birth to a new kind of war that was fought on a global scale. Instead of ending all wars, it led to larger, bloodier wars. Instead of leading to a time when weapons were put aside, it led to an increase in the use of chemical weapons, tanks, and airplanes to cause even more casualties. Instead of bringing about lasting peace, it led to greater instability, especially in Europe.

When looking at the far-reaching effects of the First World War, a nagging question remains: Why? Why did this game-changing war start, and why did so many countries join the fighting? The answer should be simple to find. The war ended only about a century ago, and we have many official and personal records from that time. Photographs of soldiers and battlefields are also readily available. However, students and scholars alike are still searching for a concrete explanation for why this conflict, which could have remained an isolated incident, exploded into the first truly global war.

The immediate cause of the war is well-known. On June 28, 1914, Archduke Franz Ferdinand, who was the heir to the throne of the Austro-Hungarian Empire, was assassinated, along with his wife, Sophie, in the city of Sarajevo, which was the traditional capital of the part of Austria-Hungary known as Bosnia and Herzegovina. The archduke and his wife were shot by a Bosnian Serb named Gavrilo Princip who—like many Serbian nationalists—wanted to bring about the end of Austro-Hungarian rule in the part of southeastern Europe known as the Balkans.

The conflict surrounding this event

could have remained isolated, affecting only the Balkans. However, it sparked a world war. The great powers of Europe prepared to do battle, with Britain, France, and Russia on one side and Germany and Austria-Hungary on the other. This continent became the center of a conflict that eventually reached all corners of the earth, including the United States, which joined the fighting in 1917 on the side of Britain, France, and Russia, despite its original desire to stay neutral.

Between 1914 and 1918, Europe changed from a continent whose power and influence had spread around the world to a continent torn apart by warfare. World War I brought about the collapse of empires and destabilized Europe in a crippling way, leaving the door open for another world war to tear it apart in only a little more than 20 years.

Why would European powers throw themselves into such a brutal and damaging conflict, and why would other nations around the world, such as the United States, join them? There is no easy answer, but the quest to find one has allowed historians to discuss and debate the nature of warfare and why people are drawn to conflict, which could provide a key to preventing this kind of large-scale conflict in the future.

*The assassinations of Archduke Franz Ferdinand and his wife sparked this global conflict.*

## The Arms Race Explodes

Historians may not have one set answer to explain why World War I became such a large-scale conflict, but they have come up with popular explanations and theories after about a century of researching the war. Two common explanations for the outbreak of World War I are that it occurred more or less accidentally and that the arms race that preceded the war led to war itself. These two ideas are connected. All the major powers of Europe engaged in an arms race before 1914. An arms race is a period of rapidly increasing accumulation of weapons between rival nations. This arms race broke into open hostilities with the assassination of Archduke Franz Ferdinand.

Perhaps the best expression of this theory comes from Sir Edward Grey, Britain's foreign secretary during World War I. In 1925, Grey bleakly concluded that by engaging in an arms race, a nation risks setting ablaze the conflict it seeks to deter:

> *Great armaments lead inevitably to war. If there are armaments on one side, there must be armaments on other sides. The increase of armaments produces a consciousness of the strength of other nations and a sense of fear. Fear begets suspicion and distrust and evil imaginings of all sorts, till … every government regards every precaution of every other government as evidence of hostile intent … The enormous growth of armaments in Europe, the sense of insecurity and fear caused by them—it was these that made war inevitable.*[1]

Grey theorized that the fear at the heart of the prewar arms race made European countries suspicious of each other, and this suspicion eventually led them to use the arms they had been building up.

## Who's to Blame?

The inevitability of war in 1914 has since been challenged, especially by scholars studying Germany's ambitions before the war. Military historian Max Hastings is one such scholar. He has stated, "No one nation deserves all responsibility for the outbreak of war, but Germany seems to me to deserve most."[2] Hastings is part of a group of historians who acknowledge the complexities of warfare, but still believe Germany had the ability to stop this conflict from escalating, yet instead chose the path that led to global warfare.

Indeed, some who knew the German kaiser Wilhelm II before the war believed that his ambition took Germany and the rest of the world into battle. His uncle, the heir to the British throne and future King Edward VII, concluded simply that "Willy is a bully."[3] By 1909, after a visit to Germany, he remarked, "We may safely look upon Germany as our bitterest foe, as she hardly attempts to conceal it."[4] The seeds of conflict between Britain and Germany had been sown long before the war began.

Winston Churchill, the British leader who played a large role in the First and

Second World Wars, took a more subtle view, placing blame on Germany, but also on the uncontrollable events of history. "Events also got on to certain lines, and no one could get them off again," he wrote. "Germany clanked obstinately, recklessly, awkwardly towards the crater and dragged us all in with her."[5]

Political leaders and historians have been debating the reasons behind the war and the nation most responsible for it since the war began. Some historians place the blame for the war on the shoulders of Germany, while others see it as the inevitable end result of a chain of events set in place by many European rivalries. This book provides an introduction to the what, when, and where of World War I, leaving the why for the reader to contemplate.

In 1914, most soldiers going off to war knew little of the reason why they were fighting, and they arrived on the battlefield singing, with a soldier's wry humor, their own answer to the question that still haunts us today:

*We're here because we're here*
*Because we're here, because we're here;*
*We're here because we're here*
*Because we're here, because we're here.*[6]

*These and other soldiers who fought in World War I had this answer to the question of why they were fighting: "We're here because we're here."*

CHAPTER ONE

# WAR ON THE WESTERN FRONT

World War I was a global conflict, but its battles were fought primarily in Europe. Although nations around the world joined in the fighting, this war began as a solely European conflict and remained primarily a struggle between the great powers of that continent, including Germany, France, Great Britain, Russia, and Austria-Hungary.

The armies of those powers clashed on two main European fronts: the western front and the eastern front. The eastern front, which stretched from Germany into eastern Europe, including Russia, was geographically larger than the western front. However, the western front, which encompassed the areas of Europe west of Germany, especially Belgium and France, was the main theater of the war. It was the location of the bloodiest battles and the most intense fighting. When the United States entered the war, it entered the fighting on the western front.

Why was the fighting on the western front such a crucial part of this war? It became the battleground on which Germany tried to prove its might against the two main European powers at that time: Great Britain and France.

## Germany's Growing Power

Although the Germans are an ancient people, the German nation was a relative newcomer to great nation status at the time of World War I. Germany had only come into being as a modern, united political state in the 19th century. In the competitive atmosphere of Europe at that time, the Germans felt that they needed to establish their empire as a world power and an equal of Britain and France—and the Germans wanted to do it in a hurry.

France, which shared a long border with Germany, was the target of both a German diplomatic offensive and a

*During World War I, Europe was divided into the Central Powers (in pink), which were led by Germany and Austria-Hungary, and the Allied Powers (in blue), which were led by Britain, France, and Russia. Neutral nations are in green on this map.*

military offensive in the late 1800s. Alliances sought to isolate France in European politics, and a war from 1870 to 1871 between German states and France secured the continuing resentment of the French toward their victorious German neighbors. At the end of that war, which is called the Franco-Prussian War or the Franco-German War, Germany proclaimed itself an empire. It also seized the French province of Alsace and part of Lorraine, reorganizing them as the German imperial province of Alsace-Lorraine. The loss of this territory to Germany was seen as a lasting injury to French national pride, and its recovery became a central war aim of France in World War I.

Germany also hoped to acquire control of lands outside Europe, seeing the benefits of British and French colonies. In 1914, France and Great Britain ruled worldwide empires made up of many colonies. British and French colonies could be found from Africa to Southeast Asia, China, and around the globe in the Caribbean. Some of their colonial holdings proved profitable, and some

## THE TRIPLE ALLIANCE

As Germany was working to build up both colonies and arms, it was also working to strengthen alliances in Europe. In 1882, it joined Austria-Hungary and Italy to create what was known as the Triple Alliance. This formal agreement between the three nations stated that they would support each other in the event of war. Germany and Austria-Hungary had already been allies, and Italy joined their alliance seeking protection from their shared rival, France.

Although Italy and Germany had no cause for conflict, the same could not be said of Italy and Austria-Hungary. Both nations wanted control of lands in the Balkans, and this alliance did not end the hard feelings between the nations. In fact, Italy eventually signed a secret treaty with France agreeing to remain neutral in the event of a war, and in 1915, Italy entered World War I on the opposite side of Germany and Austria-Hungary.

To combat the growing power of the Triple Alliance, Britain, France, and Russia entered into their own alliance, which was called the Triple Entente. This alliance was finalized in 1907, and it united the three former rivals under a sense of moral obligation to support each other in a time of war. These alliances and rivalries set the stage for the global conflict that was about to explode.

cost a small fortune to rule. No matter what the financial cost was, the colonies earned the two European powers prestige in world affairs. Britain and France exercised an influence out of proportion to their size and their populations. Germany wanted the same level of influence over foreign parts of the globe and the respect that foreign colonies had given its European rivals. To achieve this goal, the Germans staked their claim on a part of China's Shandong Peninsula, which included the city of Qingdao. Germany also secured colonial possessions in Africa, which was being rapidly colonized by European powers. German power thus continued to grow, and the Germans rapidly increased spending on arms to support the troops needed for conquest and to protect their new lands.

Other European powers reacted to the growth of Germany with alarm and suspicion. As the Germans raced to build a giant fleet of ships to rival the British—who, as an island people, had always relied primarily on their navy for defense— and an army to match that of the French and Russians, other nations raced to keep up with them. Spending on arms skyrocketed. This European arms race pointed ominously toward war, and some historians would later credit this buildup of weapons and the suspicion that they drew in their wake as the real cause of World War I.

## Wilhelmine Germany

When Germany first became a united empire, it pursued a delicate diplomatic policy. Under Otto von Bismarck, who was the chancellor, or leader, of Germany from 1871 to 1890, Germany attempted to keep good relations with Russia and Britain and even calm French fears. Bismarck, as the first chancellor of the German Empire, hoped to peacefully secure both overseas expansion and a dominant role in Europe for Germany.

When Wilhelm II, Germany's new kaiser, or emperor, came to power in 1888, Bismarck found that he was not interested in a cautious approach. In Wilhelm II, Germany had found an adventurous gambler who was determined to speed up the making of a large German Empire. He was willing to do this as much by war as by diplomacy. Once Bismarck had been pushed aside in 1890, the kaiser was free to adopt a more hostile stance toward both the Russians to the east and the French and their British allies to the west.

*Kaiser Wilhelm II, shown here, wanted to turn Germany into an imperial power.*

Wilhelm's impatience and irritation with Bismarck and his policies led the new emperor to take German policy into his own hands. He ruled his empire more directly, controlling its diplomacy on his own. So thoroughly did he take the reins of power that the period of German history when he ruled is known as Wilhelmine Germany.

In a sharp break from Bismarck's former strategy, Wilhelm's diplomacy relied on ultimatums to enemies and pledges of support for friends. Other nations would do what the German kaiser wanted or else face his wrath. All Europe sensed that war was coming and that it would center upon Germany.

## The War Begins

The crisis in the Balkans that resulted from the assassination of the heir to the Austro-Hungarian throne provided the opportunity for war that Wilhelm had been waiting for. The Austro-Hungarian Empire was weaker than Germany, and the kaiser pushed this ally into decisive action in the Balkans. Austria adopted the kaiser's favorite diplomatic initiative—the ultimatum. Austria's ultimatum required that Serbia take responsibility for the assassination and that Austrian officials would have the ability to police behavior that was deemed hostile to Austria-Hungary, among other demands. This ultimatum was delivered to Serbia on July 23, 1914, and when the Serbs refused to meet some of the demands of the Austro-Hungarians, an invasion of Serbia by Austria-Hungary was launched with the full backing of Germany. As expected, Russia—an ally of Serbia—mobilized for war. In fact, all the armies of Europe sprang into action. The kaiser had his war, and the struggle for control of Europe began.

The German general staff—the body responsible for planning military strategy—had already provided detailed plans for the war based on the ideas of Count Alfred von Schlieffen, a former chief of the general staff. Schlieffen called for the invasion of France from the north. According to this plan, the armies of Germany would sweep through Belgium and into northern France, opening a wide front north of Paris. The armies would then turn southward and sweep toward the French capital. The Germans expected this thrust to defeat France in a matter of weeks, freeing German troops to then turn east and face the Russians.

Germany declared war on France on August 3, 1914, and on Belgium the next day. German troops immediately started moving into Belgium according to Schlieffen's plan. Most people expected the war to be a short one. "You will be home before the leaves have fallen from the trees,"[7] the kaiser told his troops in August. The British, who declared war after Germany's invasion of Belgium, believed the same. Leaders and civilians on both sides of the war agreed that it would be a short conflict. They only differed in their opinion of who would win.

## The Schlieffen Plan

As German soldiers marched into Belgium on August 4, German guns, notably the giant artillery pieces made by the Krupp firm located in the German city of Essen, pounded Belgian fortifications. The thunderous barrages shattered the stone fortresses, and German soldiers quickly swept through Belgium, leaving death and destruction in their path. Western newspapers soon began condemning the invasion of Belgium, which had previously been a neutral nation, and attitudes in Europe hardened against the invading Germans.

The invasion of Belgium and the invasion of Luxembourg violated international law because both nations were neutral at that time, but the Germans felt that such legalities must be swept aside. Indeed, the Germans argued that they launched the invasion not out of choice but to prevent France from attacking Germany. German chancellor Theobald von Bethmann-Hollweg made this clear in a speech to the Reichstag, or German parliament, on August 4, 1914:

> *We are now in a state of necessity, and necessity knows no law. Our troops have occupied Luxemburg and perhaps are already on Belgian soil. Gentlemen, that is contrary to the dictates of international law. It is true that the French government has declared at Brussels that France is willing to respect the neutrality of Belgium, so long as her opponent respects it. We knew, however, that France stood ready for invasion. France could wait, but we could not wait. A French movement upon our flank upon the lower Rhine might have been disastrous. So we were compelled to override the just protest of the Luxemburg and Belgian Governments.*[8]

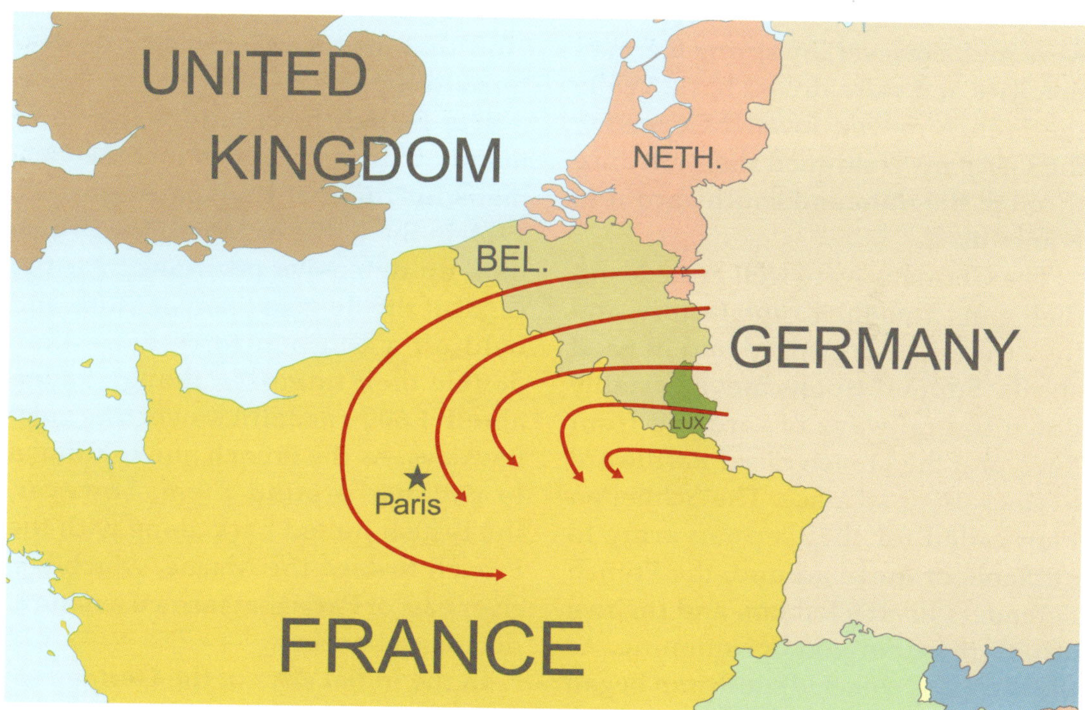


*This map shows the proposed advance by the Germans into France according to the Schlieffen Plan.*

In his own speech to German soldiers on the way to the front, the kaiser rejoiced that that the Germans would finally have a chance to show their greatness in war: "Remember the German people are the chosen of God. On me, the German Emperor, the spirit of God has descended. I am His sword, His weapon … Woe to the disobedient and death to cowards and unbelievers."[9] The Germans believed they had a divine right to wage war—no matter what international law said about invading neutral nations.

When Germany attacked Belgium, the French reacted exactly as Schlieffen had expected. They threw a strong army into Alsace-Lorraine to recapture this former French territory. They were met, however, by strong German defenses and were driven back. While the French moved toward Germany, the Germans continued their advance through Belgium and southward into France itself.

The Germans were well armed with their guns from the Krupp factory, and they were well organized and in good spirits. Support troops moved rapidly down the railways toward the front lines, and the French raced northward to check their advance. The Schlieffen Plan called for the German army to outflank, or move around, the French defenders to attack them, and the two armies raced for good positioning. As the Germans wheeled south and began their advance toward Paris along a wide front, they met determined resistance by French and British troops.

## The Allies Fight Back

When Great Britain declared war on Germany, it sent the British Expeditionary Force (BEF) to take up positions in northern France. The violation of Belgian neutrality, the possibility of the fall of France, and the prospect of Germany controlling continental Europe prompted the British to form an allied front with France to stop the Germans. "Only a menace to the very life of the British nation would stir the British Empire from its placid and tolerant detachment from Continental affairs," wrote Winston Churchill, who was First Lord of the Admiralty, or the chief of the British navy, at that time. "But that menace Germany was destined to supply."[10]

The British force under the command of Sir John French met the Germans for the first time on August 23, 1914, in the Battle of Mons. The British took up defensive positions near the canal at the Belgian town of Mons and held off a German force more than double their numbers, though taking about 1,600 casualties over the next few days. As the French line continued to collapse around them, however, the British pulled back along with the French toward the Marne, which is a river east of Paris that formed a natural defensive barrier.

In the initial days of the German attack, the Schlieffen Plan seemed to be working. Allied forces—the combined forces of the British, the French, and their other allies—were forced to fight a rearguard—or retreating—action, while preventing the Germans from outflanking them to the north. The British and French settled into an area around the Marne to try to stop the German advance. Two German armies attempted to pierce Allied defenses. General Alexander von Kluck commanded the German First Army, and General Karl von Bülow led the German Second Army.

The French attacked to break up the strong German formations coming at them. They succeeded in turning Kluck's First Army around by attacking its right flank. The action opened up a gap between the two German armies, which the Allies rushed troops into. Although the Germans were close to breaking through French lines, the Allied tactics disrupted the German line of advance. When it became clear that Allied troops threatened to surround both German armies, the Germans pulled back. They marched for 40 miles (64 km) to the Aisne River, fighting the entire way.

This battle, which was fought in early September 1914, became known as the First Battle of the Marne. It was a crucial success for the Allied armies. They prevented the Germans from reaching Paris and foiled the Schlieffen Plan. Ferdinand Foch, who was the commander of the French Ninth Army at the Battle of the Marne, described the significance in his memoirs:

> *Our adversary was dangerously superior to us in the modern war material which he had been preparing for many years and was now using with great effect. In spite of that and of the exceptional nature of the terrain here in Lorraine, his first dash*

*Members of the BEF are shown here. The BEF was formed in response to the threat of major conflict that hung over Europe in the years before World War I.*

> *had been checked and he had failed to obtain a decisive result. He had not been able to bring about that rapid and victorious march of events which his undoubted superiority in men and armaments had led him to expect.*[11]

The First Battle of the Marne provided a huge boost of confidence to the Allied forces and dealt a blow to German ambitions. The result of that battle and the Germans' failure to capture Paris proved that the war would not be as easily won as German leaders had first thought.

## Trenches to the Sea

Paris had been saved, but the Germans were by no means beaten. In fact, an extraordinary effort to create defensive positions followed when the Germans stopped along the Aisne River. While some German units began digging trenches at that location, others attempted to move northward around the Allied armies. The Allies, likewise, moved northward, attempting to get around the Germans. Both sides dug trenches in the earth to defend against an attack. The digging of roughly parallel lines northward toward the coast became popularly known as the "race to the sea." However, the sea itself was never the objective. The French commander Foch found the term highly deceptive:

> *It sounds well but it does not give a true idea of the operations; nor does it really reflect the idea on which these operations were based. The race was towards the enemy. It was his right wing that we attempted to outflank and envelop; when he outstripped us, it was his effort to outflank us that we warded off. For he was trying by increased speed to envelop us in a maneuver similar to our own. This produced on each side a race towards the northern wing of the opposing army … In this way, the sea marked the end of the maneuver, though it had never been its aim.*[12]

The trenches ultimately stretched from the coast of Belgium just north of Nieuwpoort all the way to Switzerland. These lines stayed more or less the same from 1914 to 1918. During the coming years, each side attacked the other and sometimes gained ground. Many of the battles fought over the next four years attempted to remove a kind of bump in the line of trenches—known as a salient—that jutted out dangerously away from the main line of defense and was surrounded by the enemy on three sides. However, trench warfare was most often composed of long periods of stalemates.

## Trench Warfare

Trench warfare took on a grim monotony interrupted only by the terror of an attack. Soldiers learned to live in the mud of the trenches, never leaving unless they were taken off the line for rest or moving forward on the attack.

# IN THE TRENCHES

Most soldiers on the western front lived like burrowing animals. Their trenches, which were often dug from the earth with small shovels, became home. On sunny days, a sliver of blue overhead was all the sky they saw. The trenches ran for miles, connecting with each other like roads. Dugouts provided officers with temporary offices and sleeping quarters. The common soldiers often slept in a tiny pit dug in the side of the trench.

Soldiers learned to keep their head down, running hunched over so as not to get hit by a sniper or flying shrapnel from enemy artillery. Rats were constant companions for the soldiers. The soldiers hated the rats because they carried disease and fed on the corpses that remained in the trenches.

Separating the trenches of the Allied and Central Powers was an area that was called "no-man's-land." This was a stretch of earth where no living thing grew and where soldiers rarely went. The ground had permanent marks in it from being hit with shells. Unless ordered to attack across no-man's-land, soldiers ventured into the area only at night to check their defenses and spy on the enemy. Otherwise, the open landscape was far too dangerous.

*These soldiers were some of the millions who lived in the trenches during World War I. Although trench warfare had been used in military conflicts in the past, it was most famously used on the western front during World War I.*

Attacks also took on their own kind of repetitiveness. First, the artillery would pound enemy positions attempting to break up defenses, knock out guns, and blow holes in barbed wire, which was used by both sides to hinder men trying to enter their trenches. After the artillery barrages, the men charged forward over the top of their trenches and attacked enemy positions. Enemy machine-gun and rifle fire caused thousands of men to die in single attacks. The machine guns and barbed wire made this a defensive phase of the war. Neither army could break the battle line of the other.

Manning trenches across such a long area took millions of soldiers. The British and French turned to their colonies for more manpower, and soon Canadians, Australians, and New Zealanders, as well as soldiers from the British colony of India, were fighting alongside the British. Likewise, the French called on troops from their African and Southeast Asian colonies. China also sent laborers to support the troops by moving supplies and providing other services.

These new troops fought bravely alongside the forces of the British and the French. The Canadians, for example, fought valiantly at the Second Battle of Ypres—a city in Belgium—that took place from late April to late May 1915. The Allied forces attempted to break through the German lines near the city, which was important because it blocked the route into northern France. To break the stalemate of trench warfare and stop the Allied advance, the Germans made use of a sinister new weapon—poison gas. The British general Sir John French recorded its effects when it was used against a section of the line manned by French soldiers on April 22, 1915:

> *Following a heavy bombardment, the enemy attacked the French Division at about 5 p.m., using asphyxiating gases for the first time. Aircraft reported that at about 5 p.m. thick yellow smoke had been seen issuing from the German trenches … What followed almost defies description. The effect of these poisonous gases was so virulent as to render the whole of the line held by the French Division mentioned above practically incapable of any action at all … The smoke and fumes hid everything from sight, and hundreds of men were thrown into a comatose or dying condition, and within an hour the whole position had to be abandoned.*[13]

The Germans had signed an agreement prohibiting the use of poison gas at the Hague Conference in 1899, but they abandoned the restriction to try to break the stalemate on the western front. The British and French followed suit. However, poison gas depended on wind conditions, and it sometimes blew back into the trenches of the army that had released it. Though a terrifying weapon, gas never enabled a breakthrough by one side or the other. It did,

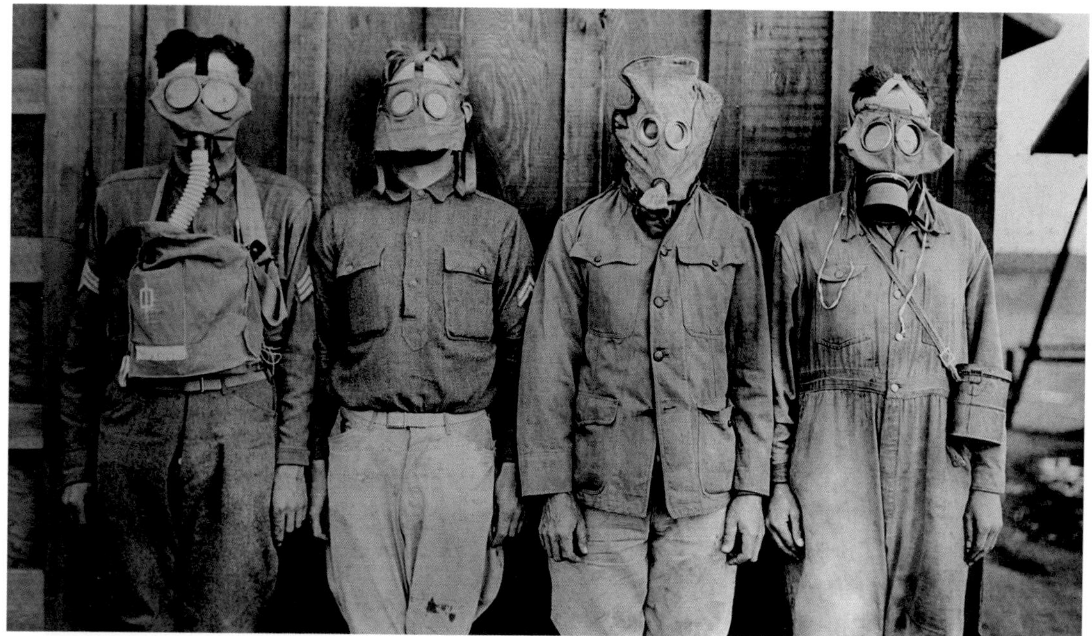

*These soldiers, like many others who fought during World War I, wore gas masks to protect them from the poisonous gases used during the war.*

however, become another dangerous part of trench warfare.

The gas mask, which protected soldiers from breathing in the gas or being blinded by it, became a regular feature of life in the trenches. It gave the men a strange, alien-like appearance. In fact, trench warfare presented many eerie spectacles. The constant shelling flattened the earth, killed the trees, and drove off animals and birds. The soldiers fought in a desolate landscape. During the wet winter months, water flooded the trenches and the shell craters marking the battlefields. Men lived knee-deep in water and mud. Soldiers laid wooden planks known as duckboards across the slippery land, and the war continued.

## The Longest Battle

Held in Belgium and northern France, the Germans attempted to pressure the French armies guarding the ancient fortified town of Verdun to the south. The Germans believed they could put sufficient pressure on the French to cause a collapse in morale. The Battle of Verdun, which is considered the longest battle in history to date, lasted for 10 months, from February 21, 1916, to December 18, 1916.

The Germans opened the battle with a barrage of more than a million shells fired at the French positions. The French were pushed back by waves of German assault troops, who used flamethrowers to burn the French out of the trenches. To prevent a complete

# THE "SAVIOR OF VERDUN" FALLS FROM GRACE

German troops attempted to pierce Allied defenses along the western front at many places. For the French, perhaps the most famous site is Verdun, where French troops held their ground during 10 months of German attacks. The commander of French forces during the Battle of Verdun was Henri-Philippe Benoni Omer Joseph Pétain, who is more commonly known as Philippe Pétain. He earned the nickname the "savior of Verdun" and was awarded the distinction of marshal of France, which is a coveted title given to France's most celebrated generals. World War I left Pétain with fame and glory, but his story does not stop there.

During World War II, which took place from 1939 to 1945, the Germans conquered all of France. In the southern part of the country, the Nazis allowed a new French state to form with its capital at the resort town of Vichy. Known as Vichy France, this new state was friendly to the Nazis, which freed them to concentrate their forces elsewhere. Pétain was the leader of Vichy France. Once famous for defending France from Germany, he ruled from 1940 to 1944 as a collaborator of the Nazi occupation of France. After the war, he was convicted of treason, though he was spared the death penalty because of his contributions to the defense of France during World War I.

*Philippe Pétain*

collapse in the area, the French rushed in reinforcements and apppointed General Philippe Pétain to coordinate defenses. More than a quarter of a million men died in the fighting. Although suffering more casualties than the Germans, the French held their ground, and Pétain was known ever after as the "savior of Verdun." By December 1916, the German assault ground to a halt.

*This photograph shows what life was like in the trenches for French soldiers during the Battle of Verdun.*

## ALL QUIET ON THE WESTERN FRONT

Fiction is often the most accessible and relatable way for us to learn about what life was like during historical periods—especially during painful and difficult moments in history. That is certainly true when it comes to World War I. The most famous account of the war is a work of historical fiction based on real experiences: Erich Maria Remarque's novel *All Quiet on the Western Front*. This novel, which was first published in 1929, describes what life was like for a German soldier living in the trenches during World War I.

*All Quiet on the Western Front* was partly based on Remarque's own experiences as a German soldier, whose real name was Erich Paul Remark, during the war. The novel became famous for its brutally honest descriptions of the monotonous life in the trenches, the horrors of battle, and the way war crushes the body and spirit of the men who fight in it. Remarque was particularly interested in writing about the difficult time soldiers had dealing with life after the war, which was inspired by his own struggle adjusting to civilian life after spending part of his young adulthood at war.

This novel is still studied in schools around the world and continues to be considered one of the greatest war novels ever written. An American film adaptation of the novel was released in 1930, and it won the Academy Award for Best Picture.

Although millions died on the western front in battles such as Verdun, little changed in the years after as both armies dug into their trenches. The war on the western front would remain the center of the storm for the duration of the war, but both the Central Powers and the Allies constantly sought new areas and new strategies to gain the advantage.

## CHAPTER TWO

# FIGHTING AT SEA AND IN THE SKY

Although many who fought in World War I did so from the trenches along the western front, others engaged their enemies in the water and in the air. Trench warfare was not presenting a clear path to victory for either side, so both the Allies and the Central Powers looked to new places to gain an advantage.

If one side controlled the seas, they could control international trade. This made naval battles an important part of the fighting during World War I. The Allies and the Central Powers clashed on the seas from the start of the conflict. In time, another kind of fighting began in the sky. Air battles and bombings from the sky became more frequent as the latest development in transportation technology—the airplane—was used in action by both sides of the conflict. World War I saw the rise of the air force as a vital military branch, forever changing the way nations engage in warfare.

### New Naval Powers

The arms race that preceded World War I grew out of Germany's desire to establish itself as a world-class naval power. Germany, which was hungry for both overseas colonies and international prestige, knew that only a navy could guard the routes to colonies it hoped to acquire. Germany also hoped to challenge the might of the British Royal Navy, which was the most powerful navy of the time.

The British navy was the envy of Europe. Not only could it defend the island nation, but it also allowed the British to maintain a worldwide empire stretching from the British Isles around the globe through Africa, India, China, Australia, New Zealand, and Canada. The navy provided protection for the sea-lanes along which colonial commerce sailed. It also made Britain a world military power that was able to influence world events. Winston Churchill, who served as the head of the British navy at the beginning of World War I, summed up the importance of the navy to the British:

> *Great Britain, deprived of its naval defence, could be speedily starved into utter submission to the will of the conqueror. Her Empire would be dismembered; the Dominions, India and her immense African and island possessions would be shorn off or transferred to the victors … The stakes were very high. If our naval defence were maintained we were safe and sure beyond the lot of any other European nation; if it failed our doom was certain and final.*[14]

By the early 20th century, other nations had begun to challenge Britain for dominance of the seas. If a nation made use of technological advances and spent adequate money on ships, it could build a great navy. The Japanese proved this in 1905. Japan had adopted Western technological methods to make its navy the equal of Western navies, and when war broke out with Russia, Japan got a chance to put its navy to the test.

To support Russian ground forces fighting the Japanese in a part of northeastern China called Manchuria, Russia sent its naval fleet on a 20,000-mile (32,187 km) voyage around Europe, Africa, India, and the coast of China. The large Russian fleet prepared to meet the Japanese imperial navy in the Tsushima Strait between Japan and Korea. In the two-day battle that ensued, Japan

*The success of the Japanese navy, shown here, in the Battle of Tsushima proved that the navies of established world powers could be defeated.*

# STUDYING NAVAL POWER

Certain books in history have changed the course of world events. One such book is *The Influence of Sea Power Upon History, 1660–1783*, by Alfred Thayer Mahan, which was published in 1890. After serving in the U.S. Navy, Mahan became a lecturer and then the president at the Naval War College and helped shape future U.S. naval leaders.

Mahan's theories about sea power echoed far beyond lecture halls in the United States. In his most famous book, Mahan argued that Britain ultimately came out ahead in international conflicts and expanded its influence because of the strength of its navies. Mahan believed that the use of technology to improve fighting ships provided the decisive factor in modern naval warfare. His book was read by leaders around the world and studied closely in Britain. In Germany, the kaiser also studied the book, and it fueled his own desire for a great naval fleet for Germany.

*Alfred Thayer Mahan*

destroyed the Russian fleet completely.

The rise of Japanese naval power and the growing navy of the United States indicated a new age of naval competition. Of all nations, Britain had the most to lose. Its ability to defend itself depended on its navy, and the British did not wish to give up their reputation as the world's greatest sea power. Once Germany decided to challenge British power at sea, the British had no choice but to keep ahead of the Germans by building bigger and more powerful battleships.

## Building Bigger Battleships

The first of the new British battleships was HMS *Dreadnought*, which eventually gave its name to an entire class of enormous, heavily armed warships.

This new ship was so powerful that no other ship on the seas could defeat it in open battle. The Germans responded by building their own dreadnought-class warships. From the British point of view, this naval arms race was a matter of life or death. Sir Edward Grey, Britain's foreign secretary, made this clear in a statement to Parliament in 1909, calling for more funds to be made available for the building of Britain's own dreadnoughts:

> *The German view of their program is that it is made for their own needs, and has no reference to ours, and that if we build fifty or a hundred Dreadnoughts they will not build more, but if we cease building altogether they will not build one less … It is essential to us that we should not fall into a position of inferiority; it is essential that we should keep a position of superiority as regards our navy.*[15]

By the outbreak of World War I, Britain had managed to stay ahead in the naval arms race. Both the British Grand Fleet and the German High Seas Fleet wanted to be able to cut off supplies to the losing side by controlling the waterways, shortening a ground war. The British had the advantage at sea, but the Germans hoped to use long-range artillery and sea mines to sink British ships while their own ships slipped behind the screen of shore-based gunfire and floating mines.

## First Major Sea Battle

The British Grand Fleet was based at Scapa Flow in the Orkney Islands at the

*The* Dreadnaught*, shown here, ushered in a new era of naval warfare dominated by battleships that only featured large guns.*

extreme northern tip of Great Britain. Geography had left the German fleet only a stretch of the North Sea across from Scotland from which to emerge for battle. Vice Admiral Sir David Beatty laid a trap for the German navy on August 28, 1914, as his British ships approached the Heligoland Bight, which is a North Sea bay off the German coast. The British were hoping to catch the German cruisers as they sallied out to protect the larger German battleships.

British ships were already engaging the Germans when Beatty's main fleet arrived. The British sank three German light cruisers and a destroyer, while only suffering serious damage to one of their cruisers. German reinforcements sailed toward the battle, but by the time they arrived, the battle was at an end. This early sea battle indicated that the British retained their mastery of the seas. However, the main German High Seas Fleet, with its dreadnought-class vessels, had not yet been engaged.

During the early years of the war at sea, the British spent much time hunting down German cruisers that sank merchant ships around the globe. This war against commerce was intended to destroy Allied shipping, depriving Great Britain and France of supplies purchased from neutral countries such as the United States. The Germans used a combination of their fast cruisers and the dreaded U-boat, or submarine, to wreak havoc on the high seas.

## U-Boat Warfare

Although the Germans had failed to overtake the British in the dreadnought race, they had advanced sufficiently to unleash a new type of warfare under the water. Because they were small and could travel underwater, German submarines known as U-boats could slip through Allied defenses. They preyed on ships that were generally unaware of their presence.

In the first weeks of the war, German U-boats sank the British warships HMS *Aboukir*, *Cressy*, and *Hogue*. Although these were not ships of the modern dreadnought class, their loss by an unseen enemy caused horror in Britain and increased caution among the commanders of the British navy.

German U-boats plagued the Allies for the rest of the war. They could pick off warships, but their true use became apparent as the war went on and the Allies relied increasingly on supplies purchased from the United States. Just as the British attempted to starve Germany by naval blockade, cutting off supplies flowing into German ports, the Germans attempted to sink ships carrying supplies to Great Britain.

At first, the Germans followed the traditional rules of naval war. Upon sighting an unarmed merchant ship, a German U-boat surfaced and allowed the sailors onboard to climb into the life rafts and float away before sinking the vessel. By early 1915, in response to the British navy's blockade of Germany, the Germans declared the area around the

*U-boats, such as the one shown here, were a prominent part of Germany's naval forces during World War I.*

British Isles to be a war zone, in which they would give no warning to any ship. Unarmed vessels of any nation would be destroyed without warning by the U-boats.

This policy ran the risk of opening hostilities with the United States, which carried on a busy trade with Britain by ship. However, many in the German high command did not fear war with the United States. "I look upon a declaration of war by the United States with indifference!"[16] General Erich Ludendorff remarked.

In 1915, the Germans announced they intended to sink the *Lusitania*, a British passenger liner that sailed the transatlantic route. A U-boat sank the ship on May 7, 1915, killing more than 1,000 people, including more than 100 Americans. By sinking the unarmed vessel, the Germans sparked an outcry in the United States to declare war on Germany. Although the U.S. Army was undermanned and ill prepared for a war of this scale, the U.S. Navy was one of the great navies of the world. President Woodrow Wilson, however, kept the United States out of the war in the immediate aftermath of the sinking of the *Lusitania*, while writing to German leaders to condemn the way they were conducting U-boat warfare. The German kaiser was not as indifferent as some of his military advisers to the prospect of war with the United States, and American protests over the sinking of the *Lusitania* caused the kaiser to halt unrestricted submarine warfare for the time being so as to avoid war with the United States. Nonetheless, Germany needed some way to strangle the British forces before the British blockade dried up German supplies.

## Stalemate at Sea

In spring 1916, the Germans provoked a sea battle that would prove to be the largest of World War I. They wanted to lure the British fleet into the area west of Jutland, Denmark. The German High Seas Fleet under Admiral Reinhard Scheer hoped to break the blockade that was pressing on the German economy and limiting the effectiveness of the German fleet. He dispatched Vice Admiral Franz von Hipper's task force of five battle cruisers to make contact with the British navy and lure ships into range of the main German force.

The British had a distinct advantage before the battle began. Not only was the British fleet larger and more powerful than that of Germany, but the British had cracked German codes and could read German naval signals. This intelligence allowed the British to fight with a general idea of the German plan.

To intercept the German warships, the British sent a battle cruiser squadron under the command of Vice Admiral David Beatty, while the British Grand Fleet of superdreadnoughts—more powerful versions of the already giant warships—steamed from Scapa Flow under the command of Admiral John Jellicoe. The two pincers, or arms of the attack, were to cross the North Sea and close in on the German High Seas Fleet.

Beatty's battle cruisers came into

"All the News That's Fit to Print."

The New York Times.

THE WEATHER

VOL. LXIV...NO. 20,923. NEW YORK, SATURDAY, MAY 8, 1915.—TWENTY-FOUR PAGES. ONE CENT

LUSITANIA SUNK BY A SUBMARINE, PROBABLY 1,000 DEAD;
TWICE TORPEDOED OFF IRISH COAST; SINKS IN 15 MINUTES;
AMERICANS ABOARD INCLUDED VANDERBILT AND FROHMAN;
WASHINGTON BELIEVES THAT A GRAVE CRISIS IS AT HAN

HOCKS THE PRESIDENT

Washington Deeply Stirred by Disaster and Fears a Crisis.

BULLETINS AT WHITE HOUSE

Wilson Reads Them Closely, but is Silent on the Nation's Course.

HINTS OF CONGRESS CALL

Loss of Lusitania Recalls Firm Tone of Our First Warning to Germany.

CAPITAL FULL OF RUMORS

Reports That Liner Was to be Sunk Were Heard Before Actual News Came.

Special to The New York Times.

WASHINGTON, May 7.—Never since that April day, three years ago, when word came that the Titanic had gone down, has Washington been so stirred as it is tonight over the sinking of the Lusitania. The early reports told that there had been no loss of life, but the relief that these advices caused gave way to the greatest concern into this evening when it be-

The Lost Cunard Steamship Lusitania

X Where the First Torpedo Struck. XX Where the Second Torpedo Struck.

SOME DEAD TAKEN ASHO

Several Hundred Surv ors at Queenstown and Kinsale.

STEWARD TELLS OF DISAS

One Torpedo Crashes Into Doomed Liner's Bow, Anot Into the Engine Room.

SHIP LISTS OVER TO P

Makes It Impossible to Lo Many Boats, So Hundre Must Have Gone Down.

ATTACKED IN BROAD

Passengers at Luncheon—War Had Been Given by Germans fore the Ship Left New York

LONDON, Saturday, M —The Cunard liner Lusit which sailed out of New last Saturday with 1,918 aboard, lies at the botto the ocean off the Irish coa

She was sunk by a Ger submarine, which sent two pedoes crashed into her si 2:30 o'clock yesterday a

*The sinking of the* Lusitania *made headlines across the United States.*

## MIMI AND TOUTOU

When the naval battles of World War I commenced, war broke out in some very remote places—the colonies of the European powers. No naval battle was more unlike the formal clash of the German High Seas Fleet and the British Grand Fleet than the battle that happened on Lake Tanganyika.

The lake lies between what was then called the Belgian Congo and German East Africa. The Europeans in those areas relied on shipping to get supplies and remain in contact with Europe. Both the Allies and the Central Powers wanted to control the waters in the area. At Lake Tanganyika, the Germans armed steamers with guns and patrolled the area. To destroy them, the British sent two 40-foot (12.2 m) boats—named HMS *Mimi* and HMS *Toutou*—over land. This trip was an improbable expedition with many difficulties. Once the boats were unleashed in the lake, however, they proved their worth, sinking the German steamers and winning the lake for the Allies. The tale is told in detail in *Mimi and Toutou's Big Adventure: The Bizarre Battle of Lake Tanganyika* by Giles Foden.

contact with Hipper's squadron on May 31, 1916, and the Battle of Jutland ensued. It was the greatest naval battle of the war and the last great naval battle fought without airplanes supporting the warships. The fast-moving cruiser squadrons were armed with long-range guns, and both fired with considerable accuracy, sending giant explosions rocketing upward from ships struck by their rounds. The British quickly lost the battle cruisers *Indefatigable* and *Queen Mary*, and Beatty's own ship, the *Lion*, was on fire, leading him to exclaim, "There seems to be something wrong with our bloody ships today."[17]

After these initial German successes, Hipper turned southward to draw Beatty into the waiting guns of the High Seas Fleet. Upon sighting the fleet, however, Beatty reversed course and drew the Germans toward the north and Jellicoe's main battle force. When the two fleets met, the Germans received a withering bombardment from the British. Confusion and the growing darkness of evening caused the two fleets to make critical errors of judgment. Although many German ships were sunk, the main fleet slipped back once more toward safe harbors in Germany. The British, despite having a more powerful armada, failed to destroy the German High Seas Fleet.

The Battle of Jutland was thus inconclusive. Neither fleet succeeded in winning a decisive victory over the other. The German fleet never again engaged the more powerful British fleet in open naval warfare. Instead, the war at sea came to resemble a nautical hunt. The Germans hunted Allied ships with their U-boats, and the Allies hunted the U-boats and German cruisers still loose on the seas. The war at sea after the Battle of Jutland took on the cautiousness of troops on the western front. A decisive breakthrough could not be won. Submarines and sea mines used by both sides made it highly dangerous for warships to sail in contested waters. The war at sea turned to a war of attrition—trying to starve the enemy of supplies from seagoing shipping. The U-boat and the mine, like the mortar and machine gun on the western front, favored the defenders and prevented decisive attacks. Churchill described the frustrating situation in his postwar writings:

> *Mechanical not less than strategic conditions had combined to produce at this early period in the war a deadlock both on sea and land. The strongest fleet was paralysed in its offensive by the menace of the mine and the torpedo. The strongest army was arrested in its advance by the machine gun. On getting into certain positions necessary for offensive action, ships were sunk by underwater explosions, and soldiers were cut down by streams of bullets. This was the evil which lay at the root of all our perplexities. It was no use endeavouring to remedy this evil on sea by keeping the ships in harbour, or on land by squandering the lives and valour of endless masses of men. The mechanical danger must be overcome by a mechanical remedy.*[18]

## War in the Skies

One of the most promising of the mechanical remedies to the problems presented both by the deadlock on land and the war at sea was the use of aircraft for military purposes. Troops hunched in the trenches could not see the enemy, just as warships had to hunt each other over vast stretches of water. The possibility of using aircraft to find the enemy spurred both sides to rapidly develop aircraft technology.

To observe the enemy, both sides made use of manned floating balloons and airplanes. Balloons were considerably more difficult to navigate and had to drift over enemy positions. However, the Germans had a solution: a kind of floating craft that could be piloted. This was the dirigible, a giant floating blimp propelled by an engine. Known as zeppelins, these German blimps carried passengers in peacetime. In war, they could photograph enemy positions and drop bombs.

## Zeppelin Raids

Although many military planners were skeptical of the use of airplanes and blimps, being attacked by air presented a terrifying and demoralizing kind of war. When zeppelins first dropped incendiary bombs on England in 1915, a new type of war had dawned. Although the bomb damage was minimal, civilians died in these attacks. Suddenly, protecting the coasts of the British Isles was not enough. Attackers could arrive overhead in the dead of night, detected only when their bombs began hitting the ground and exploding into fiery fragments.

The zeppelin raids sparked the quick development of ground defenses against air attacks. The government required citizens to keep their windows dark at night to deprive the aerial attackers of targets. The British also trained spotlights on the sky to find the airships before they dropped their bombs. Once spotted, they unleashed fire from specially designed antiaircraft guns that dispersed exploding shells to hit a wide area in the sky.

The size of a zeppelin allowed it to carry a large bomb load, but it also made it an easy target. Many zeppelins were shot down in the war, so their role as spotters better served the Germans. Throughout the war, zeppelins floated over the Baltic Sea and the North Sea, watching for the approach of enemy warships. These airships proved to be especially easy prey for aerial defenders. Airplanes could fly above zeppelins and other airships to bring them down from above.

When the war began, none of the participating militaries had an air force. Armies made use of planes as spotters and sometimes dropped bombs from them by hand, but these caused little damage. By the end of the war, the skies over Europe began to fill with airplanes armed with machine guns and mechanical bomb-dropping devices.

*Dirigibles, such as the German zeppelin shown here, gave military leaders a new vantage point from which to gather information and attack the enemy.*

## The Rise of Air Forces

The French excelled at building fighter planes out of wood harvested in France. These planes were light and easy to fly. They were also very slow, making them easy to bring down by ground fire. As

# THE RED BARON: THE MOST FAMOUS FLYING ACE

Pilots in World War I fought one-on-one in many cases. The air war introduced a new figure in military mythology—the flying ace. Because the pilots named their planes and designed their own insignia, they took on the aura of individual warriors, so unlike the millions of men huddled anonymously in the mud of the trenches. Aces competed with each other to take down the most enemy airplanes, and their exploits caught the attention of civilians back home.

The most successful flying ace of World War I was the German pilot Manfred von Richthofen, who is known to history as the Red Baron. Between September 1916 and his death in April 1918, Richthofen shot down 80 enemy planes. He became the terror of the western front and the most feared pilot in the war. In one month alone, April 1917, he downed more than 20 British aircraft. He flew a number of planes during his career, but he became associated with a single-seat Fokker plane, which had a stack of three wings. One of his planes was painted red, giving rise to his nickname. On April 21, 1918, Richthofen met the fate he had delivered to so many other pilots. He was shot down over France—but not by another pilot. The bullet that killed him came from a soldier on the ground.

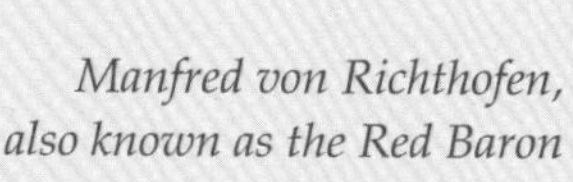

*Manfred von Richthofen, also known as the Red Baron*

planes became a regular feature above the trenches, many pilots died while flying over enemy territory.

To counter the Allied use of aircraft, the Germans developed the Fokker fighter plane, named after its Dutch inventor, Anthony Fokker. The plane had a propeller timed with its machine gun so that a pilot could fire to the front at another plane while he was maneuvering his own plane. The Allies quickly copied the technology, and their own pilots dueled with German pilots in single combat in the air. Both sides produced airplanes faster than they could be shot down, and air forces grew to a considerable size.

World War I was the first conflict in which airplanes were used as bombers. Larger planes, such as the British Handley Page bombers, held large bombs much like the German zeppelins. The Handley Page bombers, which first saw action on the western front in 1917, were used to bomb railways that moved German troops to the front. This kind of bomber flew over the deserts of the Middle East as well, terrifying Turkish troops exposed in the open below them.

By the end of the war, the British added to their armed forces the Royal Air Force, a distinct branch devoted exclusively to airpower. Although both the Allies and the Central Powers made fantastic technical progress in producing all kinds of aircraft, the air war, like the war at sea, failed to change the course of the war. Airplanes would one day make trench warfare impractical, but the use of air forces was still in its infancy in World War I. Soldiers on the ground would have to keep toiling in the trenches, even as war leaders planned for new offensives to break the deadlock.

*These airplanes were used by the Allies near the end of the war.*

## Chapter Three

# NEW BATTLEFRONTS

As the war dragged on and neither side was able to break through the stalemate on the western front, the Allies and the Central Powers looked for new strategies. Naval battles and air attacks did not give one side a decisive advantage, so military and political leaders began discussing the possibility of fighting on a new front—the Middle East. When Turkey—or the Ottoman Empire as it was called at the time—joined the Central Powers, this part of the world was drawn into the conflict.

The Allies were divided into two groups concerning fighting in the Middle East: "Westerners" and "Easterners." The "Westerners" believed that the focus of the Allies should remain entirely on Europe—especially France and Belgium—until the war on the western front was won. They believed that sending troops and supplies to the Middle East would prolong the war against the Central Powers instead of ending it.

The "Easterners," however, saw battles in the Middle East as a route to victory over the Central Powers. They believed carrying out attacks on new fronts would drain the Central Powers of their strength. They saw no end to the defensive struggle in the trenches, and they believed a new front might provide the breakthrough they needed to win the war.

### The Allies Versus the Ottoman Empire

Allied strategists believed that the Ottoman Empire, as the weakest of the Central Powers, should be the target of the new campaign. The Ottoman Empire was founded in the last year of the 13th century and expanded from its capital at Constantinople (present-day

Istanbul in Turkey) into southern Europe, through the Middle East, and across North Africa.

By the time the Turks joined the Central Powers in 1914, the Ottoman Empire was wobbly. People throughout the empire—from the Balkans in Europe to the Arabian Peninsula— advocated an end to Ottoman rule. Some parts of the empire had, in fact, already fallen away from the rulers in Constantinople. The Austro-Hungarian Empire had taken some Balkan lands once ruled by the Turks, and Egypt, which was still technically part of the Ottoman Empire, was ruled by the British.

The Allied war against the Turks fell into three distinct campaigns. The first was one of the greatest Allied disasters of the war—the attempt to capture Constantinople by landing troops on the Gallipoli Peninsula and sailing warships through the narrow Dardanelles, which is a seaway that led to the Ottoman capital. After the Gallipoli campaign, the Allies attacked the Turks first in Mesopotamia (present-day Iraq) and then in Palestine.

## The Gallipoli Campaign Begins

The first phase of the war against the Turks—the Gallipoli campaign—found an energetic champion in Winston Churchill, who submitted a plan to attack Turkey by sea. Churchill's plan was to capture Constantinople directly, thus knocking Turkey out of the war with a single fell swoop. "I wanted Gallipoli attacked on the declaration of war,"[19] he wrote in his own history of the First World War.

An opportunity to put Churchill's plan into action arrived in 1915, when the secretary of state for war, Lord Kitchener, asked his naval chief, "Do you think any naval action would be possible to prevent [the] Turks sending more men into the Caucasus and thus denuding Constantinople?"[20] The British had received a plea from the Russians to take pressure off Russian troops fighting Turkish troops in the Caucasus, which is a region between the Black Sea and the Caspian Sea.

*Winston Churchill, shown here, was the main architect of the Gallipoli campaign.*

Churchill scraped together an armada of warships too old to use against the German High Seas Fleet. The original plan called only for a naval action, but Kitchener authorized a landing force made up of British units and soldiers from Australia and New Zealand who had recently arrived in Egypt on their way to the western front. The French also contributed troops, including soldiers from their African colony Senegal. This international force was to land on the southern tip and western coast of the Gallipoli Peninsula and cut westward through Turkish defenses to capture the coastal guns guarding the Dardanelles. The British navy was then supposed to sail to Constantinople.

While the army mobilized and sailed toward Turkey, British and French warships attacked the coasts of the Dardanelles beginning on February 19, 1915. The warships' guns pounded Turkish shore positions, and raiding parties were landed to blow up forts and gun emplacements. This was exactly the naval operation Churchill had imagined. At the outset, the armada appeared to menace the Turks at will, since the Ottoman Empire had no navy to match the Allied assault. The Turks did, however, still have a weapon that could cause great damage to Allied warships—the floating sea mine.

## Gallipoli Becomes a Stalemate

Minesweepers attempted to clear a path for the Allied ships, but as the naval force moved closer into the Dardanelles— toward the narrowest and most dangerous point—the Turks were able to unleash fierce barrages from guns on the shore. This prevented the minesweepers from doing their work, and disaster for the British fleet followed. In quick succession, the Allies lost two British battleships, the *Ocean* and the *Irresistible*, as well as the French battleship *Bouvet*. A number of other ships also struck mines and limped out of the battle area toward safe harbors. For the Turks, it was an enormous boost to morale, and they settled in to counter any further attack at Gallipoli.

In April, the invasion force under the command of the British general Ian Hamilton began to disembark on the Gallipoli Peninsula. British journalist Ellis Ashmead-Bartlett watched as soldiers from the Australian and New Zealand Army Corps, known as ANZAC, landed under fire on April 25:

> *In the early part of the day heavy casualties were suffered in the boats conveying troops from the destroyers, tugs, and transports. The enemy's sharpshooters, who were hidden everywhere, concentrated their fire on the boats.*
>
> *When close in, at least three boats broke away from their tow, and drifted down the coast without control, and were sniped at the whole way, and were steadily losing men.*

# HEROES OF THE DARDANELLES

The Dardanelles, the narrow waterway that connects the Sea of Marmara and the Aegean Sea, has seen its share of heroes in history and in mythology. The ancient city of Troy was located nearby and provided the setting for the Trojan Wars, which were the subject of Homer's *Iliad*. As a natural passageway between Europe and Asia, the waterway was also crossed by the armies of Alexander the Great, the ancient Macedonian hero, and the armies of Xerxes, the king of the Persians.

In World War I, a particularly eccentric hero added his own daring exploits to the history of the region. His name was Bernard Cyril Freyberg, 1st Baron Freyberg. Born in England, Freyberg grew up in New Zealand, where he was an ardent swimmer and later began a profession as a dentist before earning a reputation for daring as a soldier. After volunteering for the Gallipoli campaign, Freyberg jumped ship on the western side of the Gallipoli Peninsula and swam to shore north of the Allied landings. Freyberg single-handedly distracted Turkish units by lighting fires along the coast to trick them into thinking he alone was the invasion force. He later made it safely back to the Allied lines and served on the western front. He was wounded repeatedly at Gallipoli and in Europe. He eventually died because of one of his old war wounds, but not until 1963.

*Bernard Cyril Freyberg*

*The work of disembarking proceeded mechanically under point blank fire, but the moment the boats touched the beach the troops jumped ashore and doubled for cover.*[21]

Despite the heavy fire from the hills overlooking the landing beaches, the Allies successfully gained a foothold on the peninsula and began to move toward higher ground as supplies and reinforcements followed from the naval armada. The feeling was one of relief and elation, for just across the peninsula lay the Dardanelles and the coast of Asia.

"The purple hills of Asia fade from view," wrote Geoffrey Dearmer, an English soldier who landed with the invasion force, "And rolling battleships at anchor ride."[22]

The Allied objective was to cross the peninsula and capture the shore positions on the other side facing the Dardanelles, thus opening the route for the navy. However, between the two sides of the Gallipoli Peninsula stretched rocky highlands and entrenched Turkish positions. The defenders were led by Otto Liman von Sanders, a German of considerable ability, who managed the front admirably. Once the Allied forces landed, he rushed reinforcements into place on the heights.

The ANZAC soldiers attempted to climb the heights and rout the Turks at night. They came very close to succeeding, but they suffered heavy losses. In the end, they faced Turkey's most determined troop commander, Mustafa Kemal, who scrambled from place to place, directing fire. The daring nighttime attack became a stalemate, and both sides settled into trenches.

## A Series of "Terrible 'Ifs'"

Life on the Gallipoli Peninsula quickly began to resemble life on the western front. Men crouched in trenches and suffered bitterly from machine-gun and rifle fire when they attacked the enemy positions. Because of the perceived corruption and inefficiency of the Ottoman Empire, Turkey had been called the "sick man of Europe" by the Russians before the war. Now, though, Allied soldiers gained a new respect for the Turks as fighting men. "On the defensive," wrote one British commander, "his eye for ground, his skill in planning and entrenching a position, and his stubbornness in holding it made him a really formidable adversary to engage."[23]

Winston Churchill, the campaign's greatest supporter, watched as one thing after another went wrong. "The terrible 'ifs' accumulate,"[24] he said. If only the navy had not run into the mines, and if only the soldiers had forced their way over the ridges, the campaign might have worked. However, in the end, it failed. By winter, the Allies plucked their troops off the peninsula and sailed away. Constantinople was safe.

Churchill bore the responsibility for the failure and lost his post. For Australia and New Zealand, whose troops were mostly fresh recruits, Gallipoli left a bitter taste, but it won their soldiers a reputation for heroic bravery.

After the failure to knock Turkey out of the war by a direct attack on Turkish soil, the Allies attempted to roll up the Ottoman Empire from its outer ends, attacking through distant Ottoman provinces instead of the capital. The second major campaign against the

*This photograph shows soldiers who participated in Gallipoli campaign.*

Ottoman Empire attempted to slice northward through Mesopotamia, or present-day Iraq.

## A Push Toward Baghdad

So as not to weaken forces on the western front, the majority of the fighting in the Mesopotamian campaign fell to the Indian army. India, which was the largest of the British colonies, was a fairly self-sufficient enterprise. It was ruled by a British viceroy, who took orders from London but often acted with a great deal of independence. To guard the colony, the British in India raised an army from the various races and religious groups of the subcontinent. The regimental system mirrored that of the British home armies in some ways. Regiments recruited independently. All these regiments were commanded by British officers. Indians were allowed to move up in the ranks slowly, though never to the highest posts.

At the outset of hostilities with Turkey, the British landed an Indian army force in the Persian Gulf, which set up camp near the Shatt al-Arab, a river formed by the joining of the Tigris and the Euphrates, present-day Iraq's two main rivers. The Shatt al-Arab spills into the Persian Gulf and forms part of the current border between Iraq and Iran. It has a low-lying delta

## ATATÜRK COMES TO POWER

One soldier in particular who fought on Gallipoli was destined to shape the course of modern history. He was the commander of the 19th Division of the Turkish Fifth Army. His name was Mustafa Kemal, but he would earn worldwide fame and the affection of the Turkish people under the name Atatürk, which translates as "father of the Turks."

After successfully leading his troops in the defense of Gallipoli and attempting to repel the British advance under General Edmund Allenby in Palestine, Atatürk became disillusioned with the Ottoman leaders in Constantinople. He dreamed of reviving Turkey as a modern state, ridding it of leaders he thought were out of touch with the modern world. After Turkey's defeat in World War I, Atatürk set up a rival capital in Ankara, raised an army, drove the Allied occupation forces out of Turkey, and founded the modern state of Turkey. He abandoned all claims to the Ottoman territories of old, separated religion and politics, and instituted a host of reforms that allowed Turkey to rise up as a proud new nation.

*When Atatürk, shown here, became president of the Republic of Turkey, he instituted sweeping reforms in an attempt to modernize the nation.*

and provides a good landing spot for sea traffic.

From this base, the British marched up the river and captured Basra, a major city in southern Mesopotamia. British interest in the region largely focused on securing the oil fields of the Anglo-Persian Oil Company. After Gallipoli, however, the expeditionary force hoped to restore British prestige by capturing Baghdad. Capturing this ancient city from the Turks was not a military necessity, but it was believed it would boost morale of the British at home.

An advance up the Tigris was authorized, and Major General Charles Townshend led the expedition. He was

*Indian forces, such as the ones shown here, fought bravely throughout the war, especially in the Middle East.*

an eccentric officer who was not popular with his men and was constantly accompanied by his dog, Spot. The British force marched in the relentless heat across a parched landscape. Townshend's force clashed with the Turks along the route and, by late September, captured the town of Al Kut, about 100 miles (161 km) south of Baghdad.

## Another Allied Disaster

The success of the campaign tempted the British to strike northward at Baghdad. The Turks, however, had been regrouping and prepared to stop Townshend's march. The Turks, under the command of the German officer Wilhelm Leopold Colmar, baron von der Goltz, engaged the British at the city of Ctesiphon, about 20 miles (32 km) south of Baghdad. The British were outnumbered, and they faced a force dug into well-prepared trenches. Just as at Gallipoli, the Turks proved themselves fierce opponents on the defensive. The British were driven back, pursued by the Turkish forces.

Townshend retreated until he reached Al Kut once again, and he decided to stay put and wait for a relief force from the south. On December 7, 1915, the Turks arrived and surrounded the town, cutting off all escape routes. Although the British forces beat off attacks by the Turks, they were trapped in the small town, growing short of food and losing men from disease and hunger. The siege lasted for 147 days, until April 29, 1916.

Relief expeditions had been stopped by the Turks, and the entire British army at Al Kut surrendered. Townshend attempted to bribe the Turks into letting the force withdraw, but they refused. "My duty seems clear," Townshend wrote, "to go into captivity with my force though I know the hot weather will kill me, for the continuous strain I have suffered from August till now is more than I can bear."[25]

Townshend did not die as he predicted. He was treated well by the Turks, who gave him a villa near Constantinople, sent his dog back to England, and later released the general unharmed. His troops, on the other hand, suffered a brutal march from Al Kut to camps in Turkey, many of them dying along the way from heat, starvation, and disease.

The surrender of the British forces at Al Kut proved to be a national disgrace and shocked British citizens at home. It added to the failure at Gallipoli, which was seen as another humiliation for the Allied armies, and Turkish pride soared. Allied forces had now been beaten twice by the "sick man of Europe." They began to fear that the Turks would continue their successful campaign right into Egypt.

## From Egypt into Palestine

Egypt had a special importance for the British Empire. The Suez Canal, which connected the Mediterranean Sea with the Red Sea, acted as a lifeline for the empire. Ships sailing from Britain to India avoided the long trip around Africa by passing through this man-made canal, and it was vital for the British to protect it at all costs. "The original object of our maintaining a force in Egypt at all was quite simple and definite," wrote Archibald Wavell, who served as a British commander in Egypt. "Its role was that of a detachment guarding a vital main line of communication."[26] That main line was the Suez Canal.

The Turks first advanced to the Suez Canal in early February 1915, in the midst of a blistering sandstorm. The approach from Syria, which was an Ottoman province at the time, was unopposed until the troops reached the canal after crossing the Sinai Peninsula, which is a peninsula separating Egypt from Asia. Once they reached it, however, they faced a stronger British force and Allied warships. The few Turks who made it across the canal were swiftly eliminated by the British, and the Turkish force retreated into the Sinai Peninsula.

The Suez Canal would have been a prize for the Central Powers that was similar to what Constantinople would have been for the Allies. However, it was just as much of a dangerous gamble for the Turks, and it also failed. Because of the threat to the canal, the

## THE SINAI PENINSULA

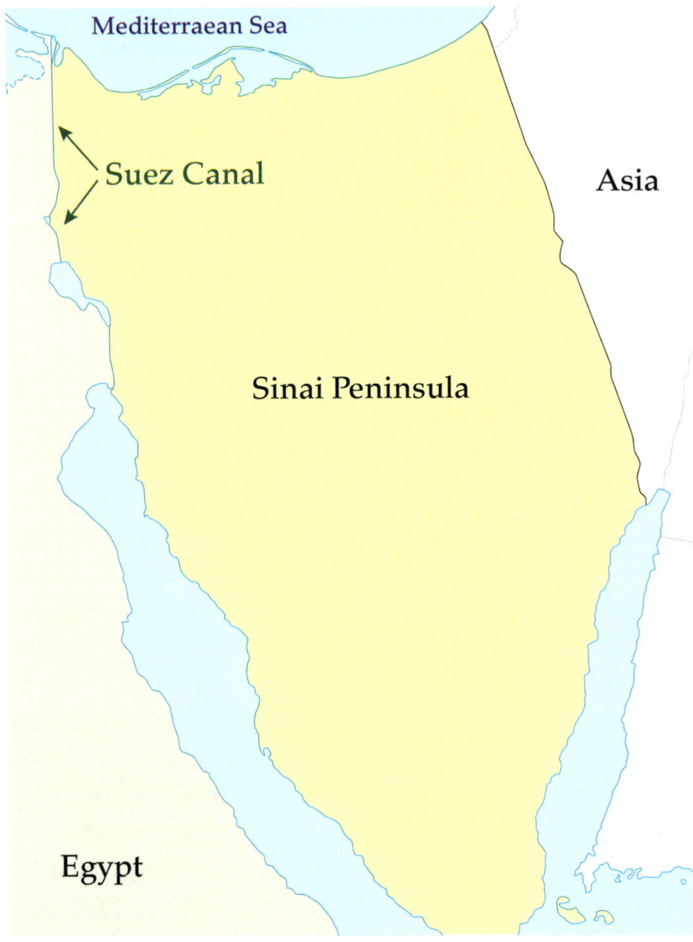


*This map shows the Sinai Peninsula. It is easy to see its importance as a bridge between Africa and Asia.*

British sent troops from home to Egypt, as soldiers from the Gallipoli campaign arrived in the area, too. The result was a buildup of Allied forces no longer facing a Turkish attack. The British, therefore, decided to launch another attack against Turkish-controlled territory. They organized the soldiers in Egypt into the Egyptian Expeditionary Force, which was put under the command of Lieutenant General Archibald Murray.

Murray led this army into the Sinai Peninsula. The peninsula provided a land route to ancient Palestine (present-day Israel and the Palestinian territories). Murray had decided that the best way to prevent a Turkish attack on the canal was to move out into the Sinai Peninsula and stop the Turks from this approach. Thus, the strategy to defend the canal turned into an Allied advance directly into Turkish territory.

### The Allies on the Offensive

By the end of 1916, Murray's forces had driven the Turks out of the Sinai Peninsula and encamped in defensive positions across the border of Palestine. At this point, the debate between "Easterners" and "Westerners" once again heated up. Murray's orders had been to defend the canal, but his success prompted the "Easterners" to advocate a further advance. The "Westerners" still argued that this would take troops away from the main war in Europe. Archibald Wavell strongly disagreed. "The campaigns of the Egyptian Expeditionary Force have been frequently termed a 'side show,'" he wrote. "If this expression is intended to imply that the campaigns were planned and executed independently of the march of events in the main theatre of war in Europe or in the other theatres, it is certainly misapplied."[27]

Although waging war in the Middle East might have tied up troops who could have been sent to Europe, it also tied up Turkish troops who would have otherwise been free to fight the Russians. Moreover, the success of the Egyptian Expeditionary Force helped to restore confidence and undo the damage done to Britain's prestige after what happened in Gallipoli and Mesopotamia.

The Allies also kept the Turks on the defensive in the Middle East in another way. They joined forces with Arabs, or people from the Arabian Peninsula and other parts of the Middle East. Many Arabs had become strongly opposed to Ottoman rule in their homelands, and they used the war as an opportunity to try to reclaim that land. They were aided by the Allies, who saw a revolt in Ottoman lands as a way to weaken the Turks.

## Leading the Arab Revolt

The British sent officers to organize Arab forces already clashing with their Turkish rulers in Arabia. Thomas Edward Lawrence, one of these British officers, found among the Arabian leaders one whom he thought could successfully lead the revolt: Prince Fasial. Lawrence wrote of Fasial, "I felt at first glance that this was the man I had come to Arabia to seek—the leader who would bring the Arab Revolt to full glory."[28]

Faisal's father, Ḥusayn ibn 'Alī, was considered the rightful protector of the Islamic holy cities of Mecca and Medina in a region known as the Hejaz. By 1916, he had declared himself king of the Hejaz, and he became an important figure in the Arab Revolt.

Faisal and his brothers had decided that Arabia would be better off without the Turks, and he provided a figurehead for the Arab Revolt. Faisal's leadership gave the revolt against the Turks a legitimacy it would not otherwise have had. Moreover, as a revered Muslim leader and guardian of the holy cities, he helped bridge the gap between Muslims and British Christians, who were both fighting the Turks. The Arabs, wrote Lawrence, fought alongside the British because, as he imagined them saying, "'What we want is a Government which speaks our own language of Arabic and will let us live in peace. Also we hate those Turks.'"[29]

Religious differences did not matter to the Arabs who were fighting to be free of the Ottoman Empire. The British soldiers were not Muslims, but they could help the Muslims acquire the autonomy they sought through this revolt.

# THE LEGEND OF "LAWRENCE OF ARABIA"

In 1917, after the United States declared war on Germany, Lowell Thomas, a newspaper reporter, traveled to the western front to report on the war. He was accompanied by a cameraman, whose job was to film the subjects of Thomas's reports. Thomas found the war on the western front so grim that he eventually turned to the Middle East campaign, where he found a young British officer aiding the revolt by the Arabs against Ottoman Turkish rule.

The Arab Revolt was everything the western front was not. The soldiers fought on horseback in the open desert, much as they had done for centuries. The British officer, Thomas Edward Lawrence, moreover, looked nothing like the mud-covered, green-uniformed soldiers stuck in the trenches in Europe. He wore white Arabian robes and a traditional Arabian headdress, and he fought on the back of a camel. Thomas had found his story. He publicized it through a series of dramatically colored slide shows in the United States and Britain, giving birth to the legend of "Lawrence of Arabia," who was one of the most legendary heroes to emerge from the First World War.

The legend continued long after the war was over. Thomas's book about his time spent with Lawrence, titled *With Lawrence of Arabia*, was published in 1924. A modern film adaptation of Lawrence's exploits during the Arab Revolt was released in 1962. *Lawrence of Arabia* is considered by many film critics to be one of the greatest movies ever made, and it won seven Academy Awards, including the award for Best Picture.

*Thomas Edward Lawrence, also known as "Lawrence of Arabia"*

## A Different Kind of War

The Arab Revolt resembled ancient warfare more than it resembled the modern, mechanized war being fought in Europe at the same time. Arab soldiers fought on horseback and camelback, raiding Turkish positions along a railway that ran along the eastern coast of the Arabian Peninsula. The goal of the Arab army was not to defeat the Turks and drive them out of Arabia, but to pin them down along the railway so that troops would be bottled up and unable to advance or retreat. Medina, which was garrisoned by Turkish troops, was the main object of this tactic. "Making the maintenance of the Turkish garrison at Medina just a shade less difficult than its evacuation would serve the interests of British and Arab alike,"[30] Lawrence wrote. The Arab army busied itself with blowing up train tracks and making life difficult for the Turks all along the railway. The Arab army was never strong enough to face the Turks head on, so they waged a classic guerrilla war that focused on the destruction of arms and transportation lines rather than on killing the enemy. "The death of a Turkish bridge or rail, machine or gun or charge of high explosive," wrote Lawrence, "was more profitable to us than the death of a Turk."[31]

*The Arab soldiers who fought in the Middle East during World War I often fought on horseback instead of in muddy trenches.*

## The Arabs Take Aqaba

One spot along the eastern coast of this new front provided an important objective for the Allied campaign in Palestine. This was the port city of Aqaba (in present-day Jordan), where the Turks had large shore weapons that could prevent Allied ships from sailing in the area. The Arab army came up with a daring plan to capture the city by an attack from land. To reach Aqaba, the Arabs marched northward and then took a detour through a blistering desert stretch, gathering soldiers along the way. The Arabs rode out of the empty land behind Aqaba on July 6, 1917, and captured the Turkish guns, which were fixed toward the sea. The city was caught entirely by surprise, and the Arabs quickly overran the Turkish garrison.

It was a stunning success, and it freed the British to land ships carrying supplies for the Egyptian Expeditionary Force at the port. After the city fell, Lawrence, who rode with the Arab forces, crossed the Sinai Peninsula and reported the success directly to General Edmund Allenby, who had replaced Murray as commander in the region. "Our capture of Akaba [Aqaba] closed the Hejaz war, and gave us the task of helping the British invade Syria," Lawrence wrote. "The Arabs working from Akaba became the virtual right wing of Allenby's army in Sinai."[32]

## The Importance of Jerusalem

Lawrence called the Arab soldiers "the virtual right wing of Allenby's army," but at that point, the Arab army officially came under the direct command of Allenby, acting as his right flank in the Palestine campaign. Allenby was then free to advance through Palestine toward Jerusalem, which is considered by people of many religions to be a holy city. This represented a real threat to Turkish control in the Middle East and the ultimate battle of the campaign against the Turks. In October, Allenby forced his way into the Judean Hills, which blocked the path to Jerusalem. Ottoman forces, advised by the German commander General Erich von Falkenhayn, resisted fiercely, but could not hold out against the Allied advance. Allenby entered Jerusalem on December 9, 1917.

The city itself, although famous because of its religious significance to Christians, Muslims, and Jews, was not important militarily. However, the Allied advance into Palestine had driven the Turks back on the defensive in Syria, relieved pressure on British forces in Mesopotamia, and secured the safety of the Suez Canal. Wavell wrote:

> *All danger to Baghdad and to the British conquest of Iraq was definitely and finally removed; practically the last Turkish reserves of man power were drawn in; and the British nation received the Christmas present that the Prime Minister had desired for it. Though the occupation of Jerusalem itself had no special strategical*

*importance, its moral significance was great.*[33]

Indeed, the British had finally avenged the defeats of Gallipoli and Al Kut. The British subsequently moved on to Damascus in Syria, with the Arab armies riding on their right. It was a triumph at last for the "Easterners." Turkey, now fearing an invasion, was forced to go on the defensive, and the other Central Powers were left to fight with a weakened Turkish ally.

*Allenby is shown here entering Jerusalem after it fell to the Allies. This city did not have much strategic importance, but its capture was a huge victory on a front that had seen many failures for the Allied troops.*

## Chapter Four

# THE EASTERN FRONT

The fighting on the eastern front during World War I was dramatically different from what was happening on other fronts. The eastern front was much longer than the western front, stretching from the Baltic Sea in the north to the Black Sea in the south and encompassing much of eastern Europe, as well as parts of central Europe. The size of this front allowed soldiers to move more quickly and easily than they could on the western front. As such, trench warfare did not dominate the war on this front the way it did in France and Belgium.

At the start of the war, German leaders decided to remain on the defensive in Russia while the Schlieffen Plan was put into action. Although the western part of this strategy was a failure for the Germans, they had much more success on the eastern front. The strain of the fighting in Russia helped create the perfect storm to enable the collapse of the Russian government and the removal of Russian troops from the war.

### The Russians Strike First

When the Germans invaded France in 1914, the Russians, who were allied to the British and French, launched their own offensive against the Central Powers from the east. The Russian assault came from two directions. In the north, two Russian armies under the command of Pavel Rennenkampf and Aleksandr Samsonov attempted to capture East Prussia, a province of imperial Germany along the Baltic Sea, by a pincer movement. Victory in East Prussia would open a northern corridor directly into the heart of Germany.

The Germans did not expect the Russians to attack so quickly. Thus, Rennenkampf was largely successful, driving the Germans back and forcing the kaiser to rush troops from the western front to stop the Russian advance. This was one of the objectives of the Russian advance into Prussia. They wanted to divert German troops away from carrying out the Schlieffen Plan in France and Belgium. The German commander, Max von Prittwitz und Gaffron, panicked when faced with the Russian offensive, and he was replaced with Paul von Hindenburg as the leader of the German Eighth Army. With great vigor and intelligence, Hindenburg restored German morale and launched a counteroffensive.

## Tannenberg and Galicia

After the initial success of the Russian attack, the two Russian armies lost contact with each other. German military intelligence had been reading Russian communications and knew the two Russian armies operated independently, without any communication between them. Rennenkampf and his troops had paused to regroup, so the Germans turned on Samsonov's army to the south. The Germans and Russians clashed around the ancient village of Tannenberg—on land that currently lies in Poland—in late August 1914. When Samsonov encountered the Germans, he threw his forces forward. Before he realized what had happened, he had been encircled by the Germans, who moved around the Russian flanks. Samsonov had no

*Russian troops, such as the captured soldiers shown here, faced many difficulties on the eastern front.*

choice but to order his troops to retreat.

When Rennenkampf heard the news from the Battle of Tannenberg, he moved south to assist Samsonov, but it was too late. The Russian Second Army had been cut in half in one battle. The Germans captured approximately 92,000 Russian soldiers, and more than 30,000 were killed or wounded. Samsonov shot himself instead of returning to Russia in disgrace.

The Battle of Tannenberg tipped the balance in favor of the Germans on the northern section of the eastern front. The Russians fared better on the southern section of the front. The Russians launched the second half of their 1914 offensive against the Austro-Hungarian Empire, which shared a long border with lands controlled by Russia. The Russians struck at an area known as Galicia, which is split between Ukraine and Poland on current maps. Once an ancient kingdom, most of Galicia was controlled by Austria-Hungary at the outset of World War I.

In August, the Austro-Hungarians struck first, driving into Poland and throwing the Russians on the defensive. The situation, however, was quickly reversed, and the Russians drove the Austro-Hungarians out of Poland and into Galicia. The Russians neatly trapped a large enemy army, just as the Germans had done to them at Tannenberg. However, the Russian advance ground to a halt due to a lack of supplies and poor organization.

Despite the lack of organization, this southern Russian advance proved to be an initial success and took pressure off Russian troops farther north on the eastern front, since the Germans moved troops south to help their ally defend against a Russian invasion. Once German troops arrived, however, the situation reversed. The Central Powers flung the Russians back. The fighting on the eastern front concentrated on Galicia for the rest of the war.

## Russian Weaknesses and Strengths

In spring 1915, the Central Powers mounted an offensive in the region against worn Russian troops. The attack caused enormous losses for the Russians and exhibited movement unseen on the western front since the beginning of the war. The Germans fought on two fronts, nearly breaking Allied armies on both. The Russians found themselves deprived of the war matériel, or equipment, they needed to defend against the German advance, especially field artillery and aircraft. "At the beginning of the war," wrote a Russian officer, "we had guns, ammunition, and rifles, we were victorious. When the supply of munitions and arms began to give out, we still fought brilliantly. Today … our army is drowning in its own blood."[34]

Russia may have lacked industrial supplies, but it did not lack manpower. Russia had the largest population of the nations at war. The size of the Russian

## INFLUENCING RUSSIAN POLITICS

Russia bubbled with secret plots and conspiracies during World War I. While the war continued in the open, a political war was conducted in secret. Bolsheviks, or members of the Russian Social-Democratic Workers' Party, and revolutionaries of all stripes plotted to overthrow the czar, while the Russian secret police, the Okhrana, hunted the conspirators. After the Bolsheviks, who later became known as the Communists, came to power, White Russians, or Russians who were opposed to the Bolshevik government, plotted to retake power.

Both the Central Powers and Allied Powers took part in the political game unfolding in Russia, attempting to influence Russian politics with money, information, and disinformation. The Germans sent Bolshevik leader Vladimir Lenin back to Russia in a sealed train across the eastern front to help take down the czar's regime. When Lenin became leader of the Bolshevik government, the Allies hatched a plot to assassinate him. Robert Bruce Lockhart, the British diplomatic representative to both the czarist and Bolshevik governments, was implicated along with Sidney Reilly, who was a spy working for the British, in a plot to assassinate Lenin. Lockhart was imprisoned by the Russians but was later traded to the British in return for Russian spies.

*Vladimir Lenin*

army made up in part for its lack of artillery and other advanced weapons. At no time was this more evident than during the Brusilov Offensive of 1916.

The offensive, which was named for the Russian commander Aleksey Brusilov, was a response to Allied appeals to take pressure off attacks on the western front and in Italy. The relentless German assault on Verdun and the continued fighting to the north caused the French to appeal to the Russians to launch an attack that would draw German forces away to the east. By 1916,

*The Brusilov Offensive—led by Aleksey Brusilov, shown here—was an important triumph for the Allies during World War I, but it came at the cost of hundreds of thousands of lives. It was one of the deadliest offensives conducted during the war.*

Italy was also calling for the Russians to draw attention away from fighting on the Italian front. Russia responded by unleashing an assault against well-fortified positions. This attack was beaten off by determined German defenders, but in June, the Russians decided to attack Austro-Hungarian positions farther south.

## An Empire on the Decline

By this time, the Germans considered the Austro-Hungarian positions their weak spot on the eastern front. German commanders replaced Austrian commanders, but Austria-Hungary was still an empire on the decline. The empire had been stitched together by the House of Hapsburg and the royal family of Hungary out of many groups of central European peoples. Twin capitals at Vienna, Austria, and Budapest, Hungary, attempted to keep the diverse empire together, though Austria was seen as the senior partner in the dual government. By the outbreak of World War I, Austria-Hungary was an empire already coming apart. Many of its subjects longed to form their own governments.

Unlike the kaiser's hungry appetite for prestige and land, the Austro-Hungarians had limited war aims. The German policy was one of expansion, but Austria-Hungary hoped only to keep its territory. Leaders feared the loss of Balkan territories to Serbia. Some Austro-Hungarian lands had already been lost to Italy, so they also feared the loss of more land around the Adriatic Sea to the Italians, especially the prosperous city of Trieste, where many Italians lived. The Austro-Hungarian forces spent most of the war fighting in the Balkans, holding back Russian advances on the eastern front, and fighting the Italians in the mountains that separated them.

## Brusilov's Blow to Austria-Hungary

Brusilov's huge army struck along a 300-mile (483 km) front. It was an

# THE "WHITE WAR"

Between Austria and Italy runs the greatest natural barrier in Europe—the Alps. They are the highest mountains in Europe, and during the First World War, they formed one of the most unusual battlefields. While troops on the western front got bogged down in the mud and trenches on the plains of France and Belgium, soldiers in the Alps fought almost vertically.

Both Austria and Italy recruited mountaineers who knew the mountains well and put them into battle during the war. In Italy, the Alpini, or Alpine mountaineer soldiers, became famous for their daring exploits in what became known as the "White War" because of the snow and brutally cold temperatures. The Alpini and their Austrian counterparts struggled to hold the highest peaks, from which they could fire artillery down at their enemy. To counter gun emplacements or fortified positions on the snowy slopes, engineers often resorted to digging under the positions and blowing them up with explosive charges, causing an avalanche and the fall of the strong points. The remains of soldiers from both sides still lie buried in the snow and ice today.

*Mountaineers, such as the soldiers shown here, fought on some of the war's most dangerous terrain.*

enormous area for an attack, but Brusilov's strategy was to probe for weak points while attacking strong points with specially trained assault troops. He also used surprise, sneaking troops up to enemy lines. Once his troops were in place, the Russians unleashed a furious artillery barrage up and down the front on June 4, 1916. The offensive caught the Austrians off guard, and at various places, Austrian troops retreated. The Russian soldiers poured through these gaps in the Austrian line with stunning speed. Within two days of the attack, the Austrian Fourth and Seventh Armies retreated in confusion.

The Russians then began advancing into enemy territory. The onslaught bogged down only when supplies failed to keep up with the troops. The Russians halted and picked up the offensive again in July and August. Brusilov had continued success, but as he moved farther into enemy territory, supplies became more of a problem, and ammunition ran low. The pauses in Brusilov's offensive allowed the Germans to move troops southward to shore up Austrian defenses. The Russian armies in the north failed to launch serious attacks on the German positions to prevent this. By the fall, the Russians had captured around 400,000 prisoners, but the offensive began to struggle in the face of stronger defenses and a lack of supplies.

The Brusilov Offensive helped change the course of the war in two significant ways. The first was the complete exposure of the weaknesses of Austria-Hungary. Not only had its armies been routed, but some units had stopped fighting because they no longer believed in their government. Ethnic groups who were neither Hungarian nor Austrian could not see the point in fighting for foreign rulers, whom they had grown tired of anyway. Sensing the weakness of their ally, the Germans took command of the Austro-Hungarian armies, dealing another blow to the pride of the once-great empire. Austria-Hungary survived after the Brusilov Offensive only because Germany held it together.

## Unrest in Russia

The second momentous event resulting partly from the fierce fighting on the eastern front in 1916 was the Russian Revolution. Russian czar Nicholas I was the first to refer to the Ottoman Empire as the "sick man of Europe," but the same could be said of the Russian Empire in the early 20th century. Still largely an agricultural country, Russia struggled to become an industrialized nation. In 1905, crowds gathered in the Russian capital, Saint Petersburg, to protest the state of the economy and the rule of the czars. The protest was put down violently by the Russian government, but discontent continued to simmer.

Russian suffering on the eastern front during World War I caused further resentment. Why did some get to remain comfortably in Russia, while

*By 1917, Russia was crumbling under the weight of social and political unrest.*

so many millions of Russians suffered and died in battle? The soldiers also viewed many of their military leaders with skepticism, and many wondered just what they were fighting for.

The economic situation in Russia only made matters worse. As Russian factories got up and running to provide war supplies, some people made huge profits. Prices rose drastically, and food became scarce, since farming did not produce the profits factories did or pay as high as factory labor. The food shortage prompted a protest against the government of Czar Nicholas II in February 1917. The czar became the focus of dissatisfaction and the inequalities in Russia. "The Emperor Nicholas II was a weak man," historian Cyril Falls concluded. "As commander in chief of the Russian armies he could not even fulfill the easiest task of an absolute monarch in war, that of arousing enthusiasm when he reviewed his troops."[35]

The February Revolution of 1917 succeeded in forcing the czar to give up his throne, and a provisional government was set up under the leadership of Aleksandr Kerensky. Kerensky also served as the head of Russia's armies and continued to work with the Allies in the war effort. However, with the hardships of war and hunger, the Kerensky government failed to satisfy the unleashed discontent in Russian society.

## The Bolsheviks Come to Power

Even after the February Revolution, there was still a sharp divide between the wealthy, who were sometimes called the "bourgeoisie," and the poor in Russia. The wealthy longed for an end to the revolutionary chaos that had disrupted their comfortable lives. On the other hand, the poor were growing more desperate each day. This desperation was only made worse by the devastating loss of life on the eastern front of the war. American journalist John Reed recorded the discontent in Russia in 1917:

> *Winter was coming on—the terrible Russian winter. I heard businessmen speak of it so: "Winter was always Russia's best friend. Perhaps now it will rid us of Revolution." On the freezing front miserable armies continued to starve and die, without enthusiasm. The railways were breaking down, food lessening, factories closing. The desperate masses cried out that the bourgeoisie was sabotaging the life of the people, causing defeat on the Front.*[36]

The wealthy hoped for a more conservative government to take shape in Russia. However, outspoken revolutionaries felt that the revolution had not gone far enough. The Bolsheviks, who were members of the Communist political movement, promised "peace, land, and bread," and many listened.

*This drawing shows Lenin on the train ride he took back to Russia in April 1917. The Germans knew it was important to get Lenin back to Russia because only he could lead the Russians in a successful revolution that would end their participation in the war.*

"In this atmosphere of corruption, of monstrous half-truths, one clear note sounded day after day," Reed wrote, "the deepening chorus of the Bolsheviki, 'All Power to the Soviets! All power to the direct representatives of millions on millions of common workers, soldiers, peasants. Land, bread, an end to the senseless war.'"[37]

According to the Bolshevik plan, Russia would be reorganized into soviets, or regional councils, that would give workers control over their government. The Bolsheviks offered Russians a new deal: No longer would the Russian people labor for the rich or remain voiceless in a government with no representation. They would also end the war and provide food for the hungry—or at least that was the idea.

Vladimir Lenin, the most famous of the Bolsheviks, was in exile during the February Revolution. He spent most of the war in Switzerland, which was a neutral nation during the war. The Germans, however, saw a use in sending Lenin back to Russia at this point. They put him in a sealed train, which was allowed to cross the eastern front and take him to the Russian capital. The Germans hoped that the revolution would cause Russia to pull out of the war. Despite protests from the Allies and accusations of treason in Russia, the Bolsheviks promised an immediate end to the war. One speaker— responding heatedly to being called a "defeatist"—outlined the Bolshevik position:

## THE POLAR BEAR EXPEDITION

Although the Bolsheviks signed a peace treaty with the Germans in 1918, effectively removing Russia from World War I, the fighting did not stop. German troops were still moving into parts of Russia, and anti-Bolshevik forces known as White Russians fought against the Russian Communists and hoped to continue the war against the Germans. White Russian forces still loyal to the former provisional government headed by Aleksandr Kerensky operated from bases in the far north of Russia along the White Sea.

Hoping to prop up the eastern front and aiding White Russian forces against both the Germans and the Bolshevik government, the Allied Powers sent a military expedition to the Russian port city of Archangel. American troops referred to the operation as the Polar Bear Expedition. Allied troops fought on this front even after the end of World War I, but Soviet forces ultimately defeated the White Russians, and the Allies withdrew.

> *You call us defeatists; but the real defeatists are those who wait for a more propitious moment to conclude peace, insist on postponing peace until later, until nothing is left of the Russian army, until Russia becomes the subject of bargaining between the different imperialist groups … You are trying to impose upon the Russian people a policy dictated by the interests of the bourgeoisie. The question of peace should be raised without delay.*[38]

In November 1917, the All-Russian Congress of Soviets, which had swept aside the Kerensky government, elected Lenin as the new ruler of Soviet Russia. Lenin advocated immediate peace with the Germans, but other Bolsheviks refused to surrender. While the Bolsheviks argued, the Germans advanced. Their interference in Russian politics had finished what they had started on the battlefield— the collapse of Russia's defenses. The German army marched into Russian territory in mid-February 1918, and the Russians knew their struggling nation did not have the strength to continue fighting.

## Russia Withdraws

Quickly losing vast stretches of territory to the Central Powers, the Bolshevik government agreed to peace terms in the treaty of Brest-Litovsk, which was named for a town now called Brest in Belarus where the negotiators met. This treaty, which was signed in early 1918, effectively took Russia out of World War I. The war on the eastern front had contributed to the collapse of another great empire, after it had already dealt a crushing blow to Austria-Hungary.

The implications for the war were enormous. The collapse of the eastern front freed German troops to move to other fronts. German troops marched toward Italy, where the Austrians had managed throughout the war to hold back the larger Italian army. Geography played a key role, since the mountains often allowed the Austrians to take up positions on high ground and defend against Italian attacks.

The Germans also traveled to the western front, generally speeding along on good German railways. The danger to the Allies was tremendous. Since 1914, Germany had managed to conduct a two-front war. Although it did not provide the quick victory the kaiser had hoped for, it did show that the German army could fight on two fronts and not be beaten. With Russia removed from the war, Germany finally had the chance to mobilize the greater bulk of its armies against the Allies on the western front.

Exhaustion and discontent plagued the Allied armies on the western front, and now they were forced to prepare for possibly the decisive offensive of the war. However, help arrived in the form of the United States, which had abandoned neutrality and entered the war in 1917. Artillery, planes, and many other industrial products needed for modern war were in short supply in

America. However, the Allies needed soldiers more than anything else—soldiers to fill the gaps in Allied defenses and to restore confidence, and the United States could supply troops.

Despite the many other fronts in World War I—from Turkey and the Middle East to the battles at sea and overhead—the outcome of the war was determined in Europe, where it had begun. Georges Clemenceau, the leader of France at the time, outlined the situation at a 1918 meeting of the Allied Supreme War Council, which directed the Allied war effort. As historian David Robin Watson wrote, "The Security of the western front overrode all other considerations. The Treason of Russia (he used the word deliberately) had exposed the Allies to the greatest danger they had yet met. His plan was to hold out this year, 1918, till the American assistance came in full force; after that America would win the war."[39] The Allies had put their faith in the American troops to help them win what was believed to be the final phase of the war, and that faith would ultimately be rewarded.

*Shown here is a photograph of the signing of the Treaty of Brest-Litovsk, which ended Russian participation in World War I.*

CHAPTER FIVE

# AMERICA JOINS THE FIGHT

The decision to join the Allies in battle during World War I was not an easy one for American leaders. The United States generally practiced a kind of foreign policy that left European conflicts to the Europeans. In the early years of World War I, Woodrow Wilson, who was the U.S. president at the time, believed that his country could set a powerful example for the rest of the world by staying above the fray and not engaging in the violence that was tearing Europe apart. In a speech delivered in 1915, he stated that the United States was "too proud to fight"[40] and that it did not need to prove its might through war.

This policy of isolationism, or remaining removed from foreign conflicts, was as old as the nation itself. In George Washington's 1796 farewell address to the nation, he questioned the need for Americans to become involved in European affairs: "Why quit our own to stand upon foreign ground? Why, by interweaving our destiny with that of any part of Europe, entangle our peace and prosperity in the toils of European ambition, rivalship, interest, humor or caprice?"[41] Washington believed in a foreign policy based on a position of neutrality, and this remained the basis for American foreign policy for many years.

By the time World War I had broken out across Europe, however, things had changed. The United States was no longer a small, struggling nation trying to find its footing in the world of global politics. Instead, it had grown into an established world power. In fact, many Americans supported joining the Allied war effort. Former president Theodore Roosevelt stated "that there are things worse than war,"[42] and he believed allowing Germany to

*President Woodrow Wilson, shown here, initially argued for the United States to stay out of the war, but he later lent his official support to the Allied cause.*

continue to carry out U-boat attacks such as the one on the *Lusitania* was one such thing.

Some Americans volunteered to fight overseas long before their country officially joined the war. They fought alongside Canadian, British, and French forces. These soldiers waited for the day when more Americans would join them, and that day finally came in 1917.

## Germany Provokes the United States

The Germans ultimately provided cause enough to swing opinion in the United States toward a declaration of war. When a German submarine torpedoed the *Lusitania* in 1915, the United States had come very close to declaring war on Germany. In the end, it was once again the feared U-boat—so menacing to transatlantic shipping—that turned opinion in America away from neutrality and toward war.

After the sinking of the *Lusitania*, Germany had stopped sinking ships without warning in the North Atlantic for fear of provoking war with the United States. By early 1917, however, the Germans were feeling the bite of the British blockade of Germany and decided to try to starve Britain by sinking ships carrying supplies to the British Isles. The Germans knew that resuming unrestricted submarine warfare would lead to the sinking of American ships, and they expected war with America. They reasoned, however, that they could prevent the landing of U.S. troops by sinking ships transporting them across the Atlantic Ocean.

To this menacing policy, the Germans added a plot to give Mexico the former Mexican territories that had become the U.S. states of Texas, Arizona, and New Mexico. The Germans hoped to stall the U.S. entry into the European theater of war by sparking a war between Mexico and the United States. This plot was hatched by Arthur Zimmermann, who was the German foreign secretary, and transmitted to Mexico by telegram. British intelligence picked up the transmission and eagerly passed it on to the U.S. president. The British hoped that, at long

## AMERICAN FLIERS IN FRANCE

Of the American volunteers who fought in World War I before the United States declared war, the most famous are the pilots of the Lafayette Escadrille. These American fliers flew French planes under French command. They served, however, as a unit, first known as the Escadrille Américaine, or American Flying Corps. The name was later changed because the Americans were still considered neutral at that time. The group was renamed in honor of the Marquis de Lafayette, a French aristocrat who had volunteered to fight in the American Revolution and became an important military leader.

The squadron was formed in April 1916, which was a year before the United States entered the war. The pilots adorned their planes with the unit's insignia—a Native American war chief. They saw combat in the Battle of Verdun, where they supported French troops from the air. After the United States declared war in 1917, the Lafayette Escadrille was incorporated into the U.S. Army Air Service.

last, the United States would join the Allied war effort.

### The Final Push Toward War

On March 1, 1917, the telegram, known to history as the Zimmermann telegram, was published in an American newspaper. Not only did the telegram state Germany's intention to resume submarine warfare against unarmed neutral ships in the Atlantic Ocean, but it also indicated that it would support a Mexican invasion of the United States. For Senator Henry Cabot Lodge of Massachusetts, who was a critic of Wilson's neutrality stance, the telegram provided ammunition to fire against Wilson and public support of neutrality: "As soon as I saw it, I felt it would arouse the country more than anything else that has happened."[43]

At first, some did not believe the news. They thought it might be a trick by the Allies to draw America into the war. People looked to Wilson to confirm that the telegram was genuine. "If the President could be got to say it was authentic, at one stroke he would be 'tied up,'" historian Barbara Tuchman wrote. "He would have given the country a national reason to be enraged at Germany and be unable to dissociate himself from the result. He had provided, gloated [Henry Cabot] Lodge, the very instrument that would be of 'almost unlimited use in forcing the situation.'"[44]

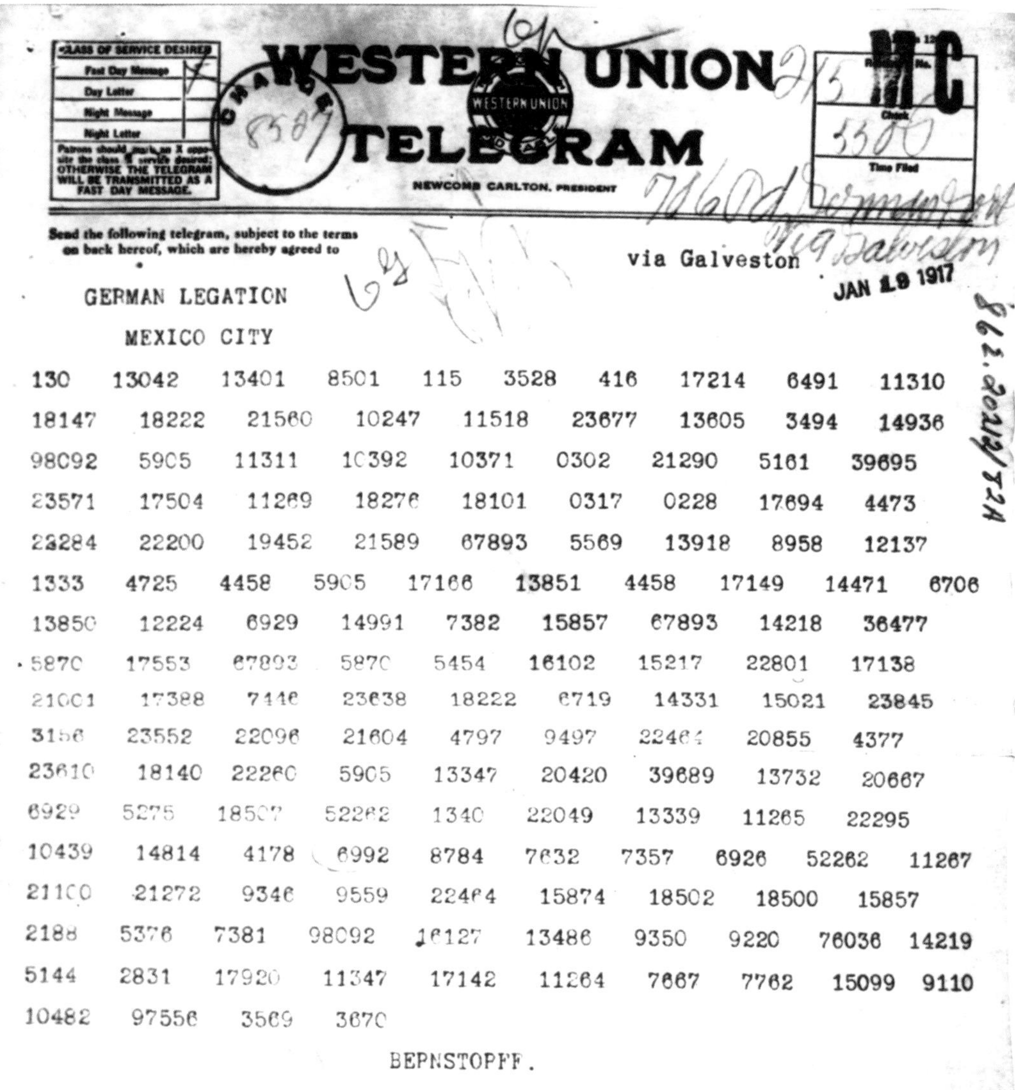

CLASS OF SERVICE DESIRED

Fast Day Message

Day Letter

Night Message

Night Letter

Patrons should mark an X opposite the class of service desired; OTHERWISE THE TELEGRAM WILL BE TRANSMITTED AS A FAST DAY MESSAGE.

WESTERN UNION TELEGRAM

NEWCOMB CARLTON, PRESIDENT

Receiver's No.

Check

Time Filed

Send the following telegram, subject to the terms on back hereof, which are hereby agreed to

via Galveston

JAN 19 1917

GERMAN LEGATION

MEXICO CITY

130 13042 13401 8501 115 3528 416 17214 6491 11310
18147 18222 21560 10247 11518 23677 13605 3494 14936
98092 5905 11311 10392 10371 0302 21290 5161 39695
23571 17504 11269 18276 18101 0317 0228 17694 4473
22284 22200 19452 21589 67893 5569 13918 8958 12137
1333 4725 4458 5905 17166 13851 4458 17149 14471 6706
13850 12224 6929 14991 7382 15857 67893 14218 36477
5870 17553 67893 5870 5454 16102 15217 22801 17138
21001 17388 7446 23638 18222 6719 14331 15021 23845
3156 23552 22096 21604 4797 9497 22464 20855 4377
23610 18140 22260 5905 13347 20420 39689 13732 20667
6929 5275 18507 52262 1340 22049 13339 11265 22295
10439 14814 4178 6992 8784 7632 7357 6926 52262 11267
21100 21272 9346 9559 22464 15874 18502 18500 15857
2188 5376 7381 98092 16127 13486 9350 9220 76036 14219
5144 2831 17920 11347 17142 11264 7667 7762 15099 9110
10482 97556 3569 3670

BERNSTORFF.

Charge German Embassy.

*Shown here is the Zimmermann telegram, which was decoded by British code breakers, or cryptographers.*

From Wilson's point of view, the Germans had indeed gone too far. The telegram and its indications that German U-boats would attack unarmed U.S. ships required action. The United States declared war on Germany and its allies on April 6, 1917.

## America Prepares to Fight

The Germans were wrong on two important points in this gamble. First, Mexico did not desire to go to war with the United States, and second, German submarines were unable to prevent U.S. soldiers from reaching Europe. By the war's end, more than 4 million American soldiers had crossed the Atlantic, providing much-needed help for the Allied forces.

The troops were slow in coming, however. Georges Clemenceau's remark that the Americans would win the war once they arrived in force was a generous assessment. Although the U.S. Navy ranked second only to Britain's, its army was much smaller. Because of the atmosphere of isolationism under President Wilson, there had been few real preparations for war. General John J. Pershing, who was commander in chief of the American Expeditionary Force (AEF), was frustrated with the lack of war preparations. "The fact that when we entered the war our Government had done little or nothing toward the organization or equipment of an army," he wrote, "not to mention its transportation beyond the sea, was a tremendous handicap which few of our people realized then."[45]

Although it would take the United States nearly a year to mobilize, the president ordered Pershing to sail to Europe with a small advance force. They paraded through Paris on the Fourth of July, 1917. The effect on morale was enormous. After years of being battered in the trenches, the Allies received a vast reserve of fresh troops. However, a fierce debate over how best to use the troops broke out at once.

## The AEF Arrives

The Americans had come, but they lacked the arms and equipment needed for battle. The French supplied the AEF with arms, but hesitated at the thought of giving the Americans artillery to use in their own offensives. "The object of the Entente [Allied cooperation] was to obtain an indispensable superiority in numbers," Marshal Foch, who became commander of all the Allied troops, wrote in his memoirs, "and it would scarcely have accorded with its interests to deprive French units of their artillery for the benefit of American units."[46]

Pershing compromised. He integrated some American units into Allied armies until U.S. soldiers could arrive in force, and then they would serve as a separate army. American soldiers first moved into French trenches in October 1917. As a point of national pride, the soldiers were determined to show the bravery of U.S. fighting men.

*American troops, shown here, provided a much-needed morale boost for the Allies, who had been broken down by years of stalemates and bloodshed.*

It took time, however, for them to become accustomed to the strange, harsh world of the trenches. "I shot six Germans sneaking up on me one night," wrote one soldier, "and when daylight came they were all the same [tree] stump."[47] Trench warfare was unlike anything these U.S. soldiers had ever faced before, and it was difficult for them to adjust to this kind of environment at first.

The arrival of U.S. troops had the most immediate impact on Allied morale. After years in the trenches, the Allied forces found the optimism and enthusiasm of these new soldiers refreshing. "The impression made upon the hard-pressed French by this seemingly inexhaustible flood of gleaming youth in its first maturity of health and vigour was prodigious,"[48] wrote Winston Churchill after the arrival of the Americans. Their military impact was first felt in a major way the following spring, when they began to function as an army and take part in the fierce

## "HARLEM HELLFIGHTERS"

During World War I, racial discrimination kept African American soldiers out of regular fighting units in the army. Volunteers from New York formed the all-black 369th Infantry Regiment, which the Germans called the "Harlem Hellfighters." The regiment was attached to French forces in 1918 and fought in several major campaigns. The soldiers of this regiment distinguished themselves by their bravery, and in the advance to Germany, they became the first Allied regiment to reach the Rhine River.

*Members of the "Harlem Hellfighters," shown here, also became famous for their regimental band, which was directed by the famous jazz musician James Reese Europe.*

spring fighting that followed a particularly harsh winter.

### From the Somme to the Lys

For the Germans, the year 1918 was supposed to be one of great victory. They hoped to punch through the Allied lines on the western front in the early spring before U.S. troops arrived in force. They intended to make use of German troops freed from the eastern front, as well as new battle tactics. German leaders theorized that specially trained shock troops could spearhead an attack, which would then be followed by masses of ground infantry. German officers of all levels would have more freedom to order offensive action to exploit weak points in the Allied defensive lines. The German army set about training soldiers in the techniques, and in the massive German spring offensive that was code-named "Michael," they set them loose.

The Germans attacked against British defenses in France near the Somme River on March 21, 1918. Allied forces had made a particularly bloody advance in this area in 1916. This time, however, the Germans had the advantage. British positions crumbled, and the Germans advanced 40 miles (64 km) before the Allies could regroup. The German tactics seemed to be a proven success, and the Germans followed up their initial victory in what became known as the Second Battle of the Somme with attacks elsewhere along the western front.

In early April 1918, German forces used the same tactics against Allied positions near the Lys (also called Leie) River, which runs through France and Belgium. The British forces under General Douglas Haig, who was now commander in chief of the British Expeditionary Force, prepared to retreat to the coast, even as he tried to bolster defenses and stop the Germans.

## The Final German Offensives

In June 1918, the Germans attacked Allied positions father south. The war seemed once again to become a war of motion, as old trenches were overrun and troops fought running battles, at least until they could dig in again. In the southern sector, the Germans made their longest advance since the beginning of the war. They had reached the town of Château-Thierry, which was only 50 miles (80.5 km) from Paris.

In response to the German advance, American troops came up to support the Allied defenses. U.S. marines—the most well-trained American soldiers—saw battle for the first time since arriving in France. American troops attacked German positions in Belleau Wood, a forest area near the Marne River, and learned the painful lessons of attacking machine guns and poisonous gas head on. Thousands died, but their bravery lived up to their pride. They ultimately captured their objective after a week of fighting and heavy losses.

The Battle of Belleau Wood proved the worth of the fresh American troops. It also helped stop the German advance. The military significance of the position was slight, but the battle helped further erode German morale. Despite the enormous gains of the Germans in their spring offensive, things were not going well. As the Germans pushed through Allied lines, they found the front only getting bigger, and they could not exploit their gains. Moreover, the shock troops that successfully led the assaults all along the line suffered heavily. By midsummer, many of those troops had been killed. In fact, thousands of Germans died in the advances.

The German tactics worked, but to what end? They possessed a few more miles of France, but they had failed to destroy the Allied armies. They lost

*This photograph shows French soldiers and a French tank on the move during the Second Battle of the Marne, which was a major turning point in the war.*

thousands of men in the offensives, and many more had grown weary of the endless fighting. German discipline, which had been so impressive for much of the war, slipped. The German offensive stalled in July 1918 after the Allied victory in the Second Battle of the Marne.

## A Turning Point

As the German offensive lost momentum, the Allies counterattacked. It was almost as if a giant pendulum had swung forward, stalled at its highest point, and begun to swing back, gaining momentum as it moved. At the Marne River, the defense against the German attack became a counteroffensive without a pause in the fighting.

On July 18, Allied Supreme Commander Ferdinand Foch ordered a gigantic attack to push the Germans back. French troops and thousands of U.S. soldiers supported by tanks cut through the lines of exhausted Germans. By the time the offensive ground to a halt, the Germans had lost all the gains they had made in the area during the spring offensive. It was a major victory for the Allies. Not only had they survived the most ferocious attack the Germans could unleash, but they also proved they could beat German armies in the field.

Foch wrote of the importance of the Second Battle of the Marne in his memoirs:

> *Above all, the morale of the German Army had been lowered, that of the Allies raised. After four months on the defensive, imposed upon us by the enemy's numerical superiority, a victorious counter offensive had once*

*more placed in our hands the initiative of operations and the power to direct the progress of events in this long, vast war.*[49]

The Second Battle of the Marne proved to be a turning point in the war. Foch took initiative and displayed his grasp of overall strategy. He ordered attacks all along the western front, probing for soft spots in the German line. In the north, the British attacked near the French city of Amiens. Tanks, which were invented by the British during the war, helped the soldiers as they advanced. Hundreds of tanks were now in service, and they caught defenders off guard. The Germans lacked the weapons to destroy them, and the sight of these lumbering steel giants approaching with a large muzzle gun and machine guns caused them to retreat. As the Allies pushed forward, the Germans fell back.

## The Collapse of the Central Powers

While the British attacked in the north, the French and American troops continued to gain ground in the south. American forces flowing into France by the thousands could now field large

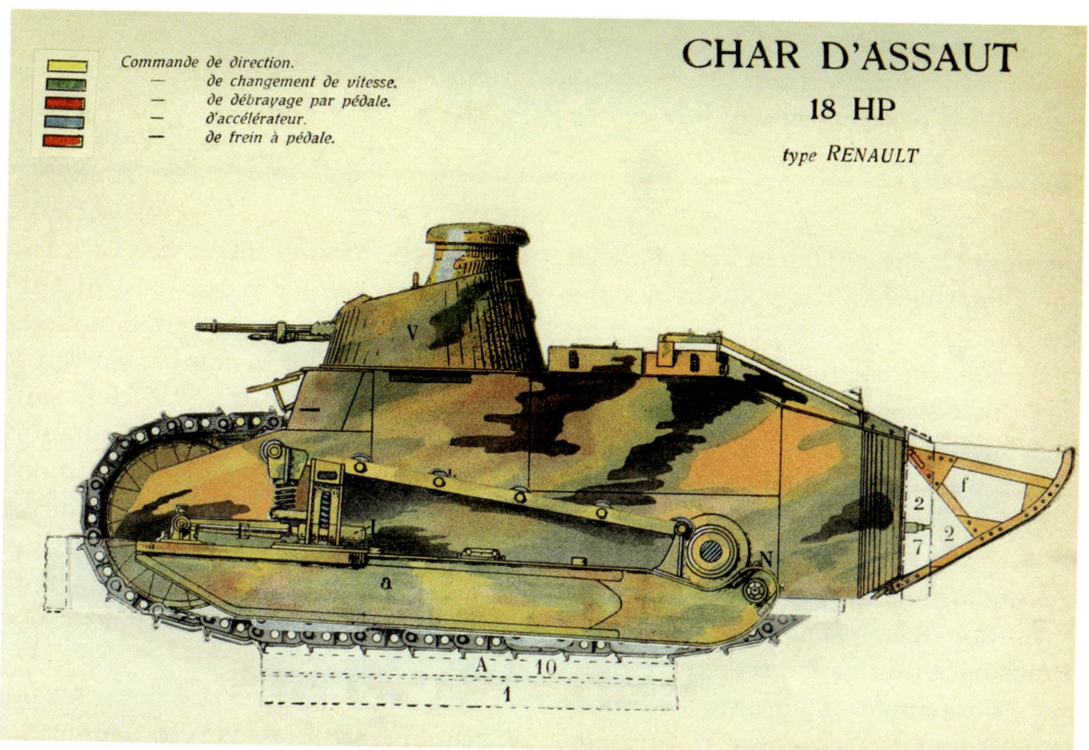


*Tanks finally provided a tool for breaking the stalemate in the trenches. The Germans had no answer for these massive military machines.*

## TANKS VERSUS TRENCHES

When war on the western front became bogged down in a stalemate and soldiers dug into the trenches, offensives became brutally costly. Artillery, barbed wire, and machine guns guarded the trenches on both sides. The Allies and the Central Powers worked frantically to develop a new weapon that could break the deadlock.

A British officer named Ernest Swinton believed he had the solution. He drew up outlines for an armored truck that could drive through barbed wire and repel bullets. The British produced the first of these new weapons, destined to change warfare forever. To keep the weapon a secret, they shipped them to continental Europe in crates marked "tanks," and soldiers referred to the armored vehicles as "water carriers."

The British first used the tank in a major battle during the Battle of the Somme in 1916. It terrified defenders in the trenches, who had no weapon to stop it. The tanks, however, had mechanical problems and often got stuck in the mud. By the war's end, improved tanks could drive across trenches, punching through lines that had remained stagnant for years.

armies. To the south, in an area that the Germans had controlled since the fall of 1914, U.S. troops launched an offensive on September 12, 1918, in coordination with the French. The area was known as the Saint-Mihiel salient, which was located south of the French battleground of Verdun.

Airpower assisted the American advance. Pershing had ordered planes from the French. The planes were piloted by Americans trained by fliers who had flown as volunteers before the United States entered the war. Pershing wrote, "Fortunately, some ninety of these experienced American fliers who had thus volunteered in the French Army from 1914 to 1917 joined our aviation, and their services as instructors and in combat proved of inestimable value to us."[50] With the airplanes overhead and the tanks battering through defensive positions, trench warfare was quickly becoming obsolete. General Erich Ludendorf, who had planned the spring offensive, ordered troops to fall back and dig in to new defensive positions.

The Allies had no desire to let the Germans rest, however. In September 1918, the British launched a major offensive near Cambrai, driving toward

Belgium. That same month, a major French-American offensive opened in the Argonne Forest, which was north of Verdun. The terrain made for tough fighting. Troops got lost in the forests, and soldiers stumbled upon each other instead of fighting in an organized way. American troops took heavy casualties, but the advance continued to drive the Germans northward in October. "The period of the battle from October 1st to the 11th involved the heaviest strain on the army and on me,"[51] Pershing wrote.

One of the great problems for an army advancing quickly on a retreating army was the ease of an ambush. German units could stop, set up machine guns and artillery, and hold off attackers as the rest of the army slipped farther away. In fact, Foch's greatest anxiety during the successful Allied offensives of the fall of 1918 was that the German army would fall back and regroup, and the static trench warfare would start again:

> *Ever since the middle of the month of August [1918] I had been worried by the fear that the German Commander in Chief might extricate his armies from our grip and abruptly break off the combat in order to resume it some distance in the rear. Here he could select better positions on a shorter front, behind obstacles and on ground more favourable to the defensive and make a new distribution of his forces such as might enable him to launch an advantageous counter attack.*[52]

In October 1918, the Allied armies advanced in three prongs—north, center, and south—along the western front. After lingering for so long in the trenches, the armies closed in on Germany itself. At this point, political factors took over. The Ottoman Empire surrendered in October. Austria-Hungary split apart. The Italians advanced into land long held by Austrian forces, and the various peoples of Austria-Hungary declared their independence from the crumbling empire. The Austrians—at the heart of the empire—surrendered to the Italians in the first week of November. The Hungarians ended their ancient association with Austria, declaring their independence and surrendering to the Allies. Everywhere, it seemed, the Central Powers were collapsing.

## The Armistice

This was no less true in Germany. Hunger and war weariness stalked the German people. They took to the streets in protest against the kaiser and his war. New political parties called for an end to the German Empire and the founding of a German republic. Many soldiers had also had enough. When Admiral Hipper ordered the German High Seas Fleet out in the autumn of 1918, the sailors mutinied. There would be no more fighting at sea.

The army held, though. It was not ready to surrender its pride. The kaiser, on the other hand, lost his nerve. On November 10, 1918, he fled to the Netherlands, where he lived in exile for

*The surrender of Germany and the end of World War I were celebrated in many parts of the world, including the United States, as shown in this photograph.*

the rest of his life. His ambition to make the German Empire the equal of Great Britain and to win fame as a great war leader had led only to ruin in Germany and the end of the German monarchy. Revolution was in the air, and Germany's new leaders scrambled to put together a more moderate government.

The day after the kaiser abandoned Germany, a German delegation traveled to France to sign the document that would officially end the war. At 11 a.m., guns all along the western front fell silent. For France, where so much of the fighting had taken place, it was a bittersweet moment. They had won, and they would regain their beloved lands of Alsace and Lorraine. They had avenged the defeat of 1871, but large swaths of French territory were a wasteland.

There would be little sympathy for Germany in the peace negotiations that were held the following year on the outskirts of Paris. French leader Georges Clemenceau believed that a harsh peace should follow Germany's brutal war: "The most terrible balancing of accounts between peoples has begun. The account will be paid … Our dead gave their blood in witness that we took up the greatest challenge ever offered to the laws of civilized humanity. Let it be then, as Germany has willed it, as Germany has made it."[53] The French wanted Germany to pay for the damage the war had done, and that attitude strongly influenced the peace negotiations in France.

EPILOGUE

# "A PEACE TO END PEACE"

World War I was a devastating conflict. It is believed that more than 8.5 million soldiers died in the war and more than 20 million more were wounded. Civilians also suffered greatly during this conflict, and it is believed that more than 13 million of them lost their lives. However, it is difficult to find accurate numbers of the dead and wounded during this time because official records did not exist in many countries.

One of the reasons it is difficult to know exactly how many people were killed or injured during World War I is the instability the war caused. Four major empires—the German, Austro-Hungarian, Russian, and Ottoman Empires—had been destroyed by the time the war was over. This was a war of great losses—loss of life, loss of land, loss of political power, and loss of economic stability. When the soldiers returned home from the front, they, too, were lost. In fact, many referred to the generation who came of age during World War I as the "lost generation."

The peace negotiations that followed World War I attempted to make up for some of these losses and secure peace across war-torn Europe. However, as Archibald Wavell stated, "After the 'war to end war,' they seem to have been pretty successful in Paris at making a 'Peace to end Peace.'"[54] Instead of ending this period of global conflict, the fallout from World War I ensured that it would continue.

## Peace Talks in Paris

The Paris Peace Conference, which lasted from January 1919 to January 1920, was the formal name for the peace talks following World War I. Delegations from around the world traveled to Paris. The victorious Allies,

*The leaders of the "Big Four" (Italy, France, Britain, and the United States) are shown here. Woodrow Wilson is on the far right in this photograph.*

beaten. Nevertheless, they believed they would be able to argue their case in Paris. This did not happen. The decisions made in Paris were made by the Allied Powers alone. The Germans were not consulted.

Why, then, did it take so long for the Allies to reach acceptable peace terms? The Allied Powers had very different ideas of how the world should look after the war. The great drama of the peace negotiations played out not between the Allied and Central Powers— the victors and the vanquished—but among the Allies themselves.

France, Britain, and the United States formed the "Big Three" of the negotiations in Paris. Italy, which was at times included with the three great powers, sometimes made for a "Big Four." The leaders of these nations made the main decisions at this peace conference.

## The Fourteen Points

When the Germans agreed to an armistice, they had based their hopes on the principles of U.S. president Woodrow Wilson. After avoiding war until 1917, Wilson declared before a joint session of the U.S. Congress that the world

who controlled the proceedings, perhaps came as close to forming a world government as has ever been seen in history. They drew up new maps for parts of Europe, Asia, Africa, and the Middle East. They listened to the delegations arguing their positions and ruled on them like judges in a court. Sometimes they made rulings based on fairness, sometimes on logic, and sometimes on emotion alone. At times, they made decisions that would benefit only themselves.

When the Germans agreed to the armistice on November 11, 1918, they believed they had agreed to negotiate peace terms. They thought they would argue over the future of Germany, though admittedly from the position of a country whose leaders had been must be made safe for democracy:

> *We shall fight for the things which we have always carried nearest our hearts—for democracy, for the right of those who submit to authority to have a voice in their own governments, for the rights and liberties of small nations, for a universal dominion of right by such a concert of free peoples as shall bring peace and safety to all nations and make the world itself at last free.*[55]

These were noble ideas befitting the American republic, which had fought for its own democratic rights and won independence from the British Empire through revolution.

Wilson outlined his ambitions for world peace in 1918 in his famous Fourteen Points. Above all, Wilson emphasized that the future of the peoples of the world should be determined by those peoples themselves. Wilson believed the Allies would help bring peace and self-government to the new nations that formed following the war. Political boundaries would be redrawn to represent only the wishes of the citizens of those countries.

Some of the Fourteen Points were very specific. Wilson believed the ancient state of Poland, which had been controlled by the Austro-Hungarian Empire, should reemerge as an independent country. Also, all troops should leave Belgium, the invasion of which had outraged the world in 1914.

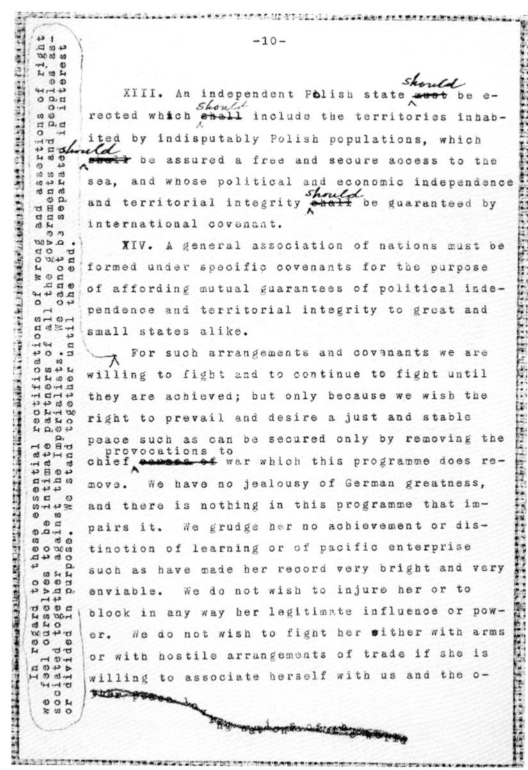

-10-

XIII. An independent Polish state ~~must~~ should be erected which ~~shall~~ should include the territories inhabited by indisputably Polish populations, which ~~shall~~ should be assured a free and secure access to the sea, and whose political and economic independence and territorial integrity ~~shall~~ should be guaranteed by international covenant.

XIV. A general association of nations must be formed under specific covenants for the purpose of affording mutual guarantees of political independence and territorial integrity to great and small states alike.

In regard to these essential rectifications of wrong and assertions of right we feel ourselves to be intimate partners of all the governments and peoples associated together against the Imperialists. We cannot be separated in interest or divided in purpose. We stand together until the end.

For such arrangements and covenants we are willing to fight and to continue to fight until they are achieved; but only because we wish the right to prevail and desire a just and stable peace such as can be secured only by removing the chief ~~causes of~~ provocations to war which this programme does remove. We have no jealousy of German greatness, and there is nothing in this programme that impairs it. We grudge her no achievement or distinction of learning or of pacific enterprise such as have made her record very bright and very enviable. We do not wish to injure her or to block in any way her legitimate influence or power. We do not wish to fight her either with arms or with hostile arrangements of trade if she is willing to associate herself with us and the o-

*Shown here is part of Wilson's original speech that contained his Fourteen Points for peace.*

Other points were deceptively simple. In point five, Wilson called for "a free, open-minded, and absolutely impartial adjustment of all colonial claims."[56] What exactly did that mean? Were all colonies to be granted independence as newly formed countries?

The Allies debated the practicality of Wilson's Fourteen Points, but on his arrival in Paris, he was hailed almost as a prophet. All the hope and optimism for a new world order seemed to be placed on the shoulders of the American president. They cheered him in France and in newspapers around the world. The

## COLONEL EDWARD HOUSE

The Paris Peace Conference welcomed advisers and experts from around the world. For the most part, the negotiations were directed by the leaders of France, Great Britain, Italy, and the United States. Each nation's leader was accompanied by experts in foreign affairs. The American delegation included Robert Lansing, who was the secretary of state, or director of U.S. foreign policy. Lansing soon found, however, that his advice was often ignored and that President Woodrow Wilson listened instead to another adviser, who held no official government post in the United States. This was Colonel Edward M. House.

House, who was always known as Colonel House even though he was not a colonel, had backed Wilson for president. After Wilson was elected, House became his closest adviser and even lived in the White House. House became a major international figure and a leading negotiator for the U.S. delegation to the Paris Peace Conference. He and Wilson grew apart toward the end of the conference because of their differences concerning the treaty terms, and their friendship came to an end.

Americans offered a new way of ordering world affairs.

According to Wilson's ideas, countries would be redrawn on the map by language groups or ethnic groups. The Austro-Hungarian Empire had already broken into two separate countries, Austria and Hungary. From the ruins of that empire, other nations emerged: Czechoslovakia, Poland, Ukraine, and Balkan nations. Likewise, from the old Ottoman lands in the Middle East, new Arab countries arose, free at last to determine their own future.

### Conflicting Plans for Colonies

Wilson's plan, however, was not wholeheartedly supported by the other Allied Powers. Britain and France still had empires to run, and Italy had joined the Allied cause with no greater objective than seizing more land for itself. If the British and French were to adopt Wilson's program, what would happen to their empires? The French and British also considered the United States to be a latecomer to the war effort. While they needed U.S. troops in the war, they hardly welcomed Wilson's suggestion that colonies should be given a choice to form independent nations.

Traditionally, lands seized from a nation defeated at war were divided between the victors. Wilson wanted none of this. The British and the French, however, had started dividing up the spoils of war even before the war ended. After

*King George V of Britain, shown here, believed Britain and France had the right to lands in the Middle East because they won the war.*

taking power in Russia, the Bolsheviks published secret treaties signed by the British and French dividing the Middle East between themselves. The Sykes-Picot Agreement—the secret agreement to divide former Ottoman lands—was meant to give Britain power in Mesopotamia (present-day Iraq), Palestine (present-day Israel and the Palestinian territories), and Jordan; France was to be granted power in the lands of Syria, including Lebanon, and part of Turkey. For the French and British, land in the Middle East was seen as the just prize for winning the war.

A British officer serving in the Palestine campaign concluded after meeting with King George V that the king had no intention of relinquishing land captured from the Central Powers. The officer stated, "He [King George V] seemed to take it for granted that German East Africa, Palestine and Mesopotamia would come under the British Crown at the end of the war ... He particularly desired Palestine for biblical reasons. He made some remarks about the final crusade."[57]

These secret agreements went against Wilson's plan for peace. He explicitly called for "open covenants of peace, openly arrived at,"[58] in the first of his Fourteen Points. The secret treaties also contradicted wartime guarantees of the Allied Powers. For example, on November 7, 1918, the British and French published a joint statement concerning their intention to support independent governments in the Middle East:

> *The goal envisaged by France and Great Britain in prosecuting in the East the war set in train by the German ambition is the complete and final liberation of the peoples who have for so long been oppressed by the Turks, and the setting up of national governments and administrations that shall derive their authority from the free exercise of the initiative and choice of the indigenous populations.*[59]

The Allies, especially Britain and France, appeared to be contradicting themselves—at once promising independence for new nations and hoping to expand their own influence through new colonies.

## Wilson Compromises

There was a single point among Wilson's Fourteen Points that he held more dearly than all the others. It was the last on his list, and it called for an association of nations to guarantee the rights of smaller nations in the future and to prevent war. This association was named the League of Nations. In Wilson's view, the war had been caused by secret treaties, greed, and the bullying of larger powers. The League of Nations would prevent future wars by openly protecting smaller nations and settling international disputes. It was a radical, far-thinking idea.

The French leader, Georges Clemenceau, and the British prime minister, David Lloyd George, realized how much Wilson cared about the League of Nations plan. Both leaders showed considerably more skill at the give and take of debate. They used Wilson's attachment to the plan to get him to compromise on other subjects. The peace conference became a grand haggling over the future of large parts of the globe. Wilson agreed, for example, to the division of influence between Britain and France in the Middle East, but only if the territories would be governed under the League of Nations. By this plan, the British and French would have a League of Nations mandate to guide the new nations toward

## THE MODERN MIDDLE EAST TAKES SHAPE

The collapse of the Ottoman Empire left huge areas of the Middle East without an established government. Turkey, which was the center of the former Ottoman Empire, became a republic and abandoned all claims to Middle Eastern lands.

The map of the Middle East that we know today was drawn up by the French and British in the years following World War I. The French controlled the ancient Roman province of Syria, and eventually, Lebanon broke away and formed its own independent country. The British awarded the Hashemite family—their wartime ally—the kingdoms of Trans-Jordan (present-day Jordan), which was also known as Transjordan, and Iraq, though the Hashemite leader of Iraq, King Faisal, was later overthrown. In the heart of Arabia, a Muslim leader named Ibn Sa'ūd founded his own nation, which is known today as Saudi Arabia.

## GLOBAL GROUPS FOR PEACE

Despite all of Wilson's compromises, the U.S. Congress rejected the Treaty of Versailles, and the United States did not join the League of Nations. However, Wilson's dream of creating an international body to settle disputes between nations lived on after him. The League of Nations was officially formed—without the United States—in 1920. However, this body was not strong enough to work toward world peace.

The League of Nations ultimately failed to stop the increasing aggression of the 1930s. It took another world war to convince the world that such a body was in the common interest. The league lingered on until 1946. By then a new organization, which was known as the United Nations (UN), had begun to facilitate international security after its founding in October 1945. Today, the UN plays an active role in settling international disputes around the globe.

*UN headquarters in New York City*

self-government. Wilson, in fact, was agreeing to new colonies under a different name.

The Arabs, who had fought alongside the Allies against the Turks, felt betrayed. Some of the British officers who served with them felt ashamed of Britain's treatment of their wartime ally. "We lived many lives in those whirling campaigns, never sparing ourselves: yet when we achieved and the new world dawned, the old men came out again and took our victory to remake in the likeness of the former world they knew,"[60] wrote Thomas Edward Lawrence.

As the peace conference progressed, Wilson conceded to ever more trade-offs to retain support for the League of Nations. It was as if the U.S. president sacrificed the short term for the future. He hoped the League of Nations would prevent war and mark a new age of international relations. In the short term, compromises had to be made.

## Conflicting Claims to Qingdao

Nowhere was Wilson's compromising more apparent than the debate over the Chinese province of Shandong. Japanese delegates joined the Council of Ten, which was the main decision-making body at the peace negotiations, as equals of the other great powers—France, Great Britain, the United States, and Italy (each had two delegates, making for a council of 10 members). Japan was a rising power with a strong navy. The Japanese had played only a minor role in the war, but to secure their support for a League of Nations, Wilson agreed to their demands in Paris.

The Japanese wanted the former German colony of Qingdao on the Shandong Peninsula. The Chinese, of course, wanted their territory back. Not only did the Chinese have the legal claim to the area, since it was indisputably part of China, but they had also supported the Allied Powers in the war. Chinese workers sailed from the Far East and supported Allied troops on the western front by working behind the lines, helping transport supplies. The Chinese responded to the Japanese claim to Shandong with outrage.

American opinion generally sided with the Chinese, and even members of the American delegation at the peace conference believed the United States could not, in good faith, agree to the Japanese demand. General Tasker H. Bliss, who was a member of the American delegation, wrote in a letter to

*Members of the Chinese Labour Corps, such as those shown here, provided support to the Allied troops during World War I. However, the Allies did not support China's attempt to take back its land on the Shandong Peninsula after the war.*

President Wilson:

> *If we support Japan's claim, we abandon the democracy of China to the domination of the Prussianized militarism of Japan.*
>
> *We shall be sowing dragons' teeth.*
>
> *It can't be right to do wrong even to make peace. Peace is desirable, but there are things dearer than peace, justice and freedom.*[61]

Robert Lansing, who was the U.S. secretary of state and a peace commissioner on the American delegation to Paris, believed that Wilson was sacrificing basic U.S. principles to secure support for the League of Nations. In his 1921 account of the peace negotiations, he wrote:

> *Our chief differences were, first, that it was more important to insure the acceptance of the Covenant of the League of Nations than to do strict justice to China; second, that the Japanese withdrawal from the Conference would prevent the formation of the League; and, third, that Japan would have withdrawn if her claims had been denied.*[62]

Japan, however, eventually won support for its possession of Chinese territory. In later years, the Japanese moved farther into Chinese territory and eventually attempted to dominate China entirely. In China, the Treaty of Versailles was treated as evidence that the Western powers would support a fellow military power over a fellow democracy.

World War I had eroded the admiration of Western civilization all over the world. The peace treaty that followed further undermined the credibility of the West among nations in East Asia, the Middle East, and Africa.

## New Lands

Despite the anticolonial nature of Wilson's Fourteen Points, he compromised on most of the colonial questions, and both the French and British empires expanded after the war. The Japanese Empire, which the Allied Powers later fought in World War II, also grew in strength and territory from the peace terms decided in Paris in 1919.

However, because of the open discussions on colonies and because of Wilson's support for self-determination—the right of people everywhere to decide what kind of government they wanted—discontent in colonies around the globe grew steadily. World War I is thus often credited with helping to bring about the end of the colonial system.

In Europe, the collapse of the Austro-Hungarian Empire and the Ottoman Empire allowed many countries to form their own government. For example, Poland, which had been controlled by foreign powers for so long, reemerged as an independent country.

An army of linguists, mapmakers, and historians attempted to regroup people into new nations based on common language and ethnicity.

## Punishing Germany

When the Allies took up the question of Germany, disputes among the Big Three once again flared up. The future of Germany—the cause of so much suffering in this global conflict—sparked a fierce debate. The French, who shared a border with Germany and had been invaded by the Germans, wanted Germany to be treated harshly. The French also wanted to make sure the German army could not strike again.

Above all, two factors proved difficult to agree upon. France wanted the Allies to occupy the Rhineland, which was part of Germany that bordered France, and it wanted Germany to pay for the war. According to the French, the Germans needed to be demilitarized. Their army needed to be reduced to a small force, and no submarines or warplanes would be allowed if the French had their way. French leaders believed the safety of France could only be ensured through the occupation of German territory and the disbanding of the German military. "America is far away, protected by the ocean. Even Napoleon could not reach England," Clemenceau argued to Wilson and Lloyd George. "You are both under cover. We are not. No man has less of the militaristic spirit than I. But we want safety."[63] The British and Americans agreed, principally out of respect for France.

*The harsh terms of the Treaty of Versailles led to great resentment and anger in Germany. Adolf Hitler, shown here, capitalized on this resentment as he rose to power. Hitler's Nazi Germany would then become the center of another global conflict: World War II.*

The Allies also wanted the Germans to repay the costs of the war in payments known as reparations. Great Britain, however, feared that the European economy would suffer if Germany were crippled with war debt. The United States also hoped that the German economy would get up and running as soon as possible. Wilson had called for a peace without victory as the war aim of the United States. He took the long view that a strong, democratic Germany would make war in Europe less likely in the future.

The Allies could not agree on the

amount, but it was clear that the Germans would be required to pay much in reparations to the Allied Powers over the coming years. The question of the specifics concerning reparations was ultimately put off for a later convention. This made the Germans extremely uneasy. They were signing a document that required them to pay their enemies an undetermined amount of money over an undetermined period of time. "The German people would thus be condemned to perpetual slave labour,"[64] remarked one of the German delegates to the peace conference.

Although the Germans were unhappy with the terms of the treaty, which called for them to take full blame for the conflict, they had no choice but to accept them. From the Allied point of view, Germany either had to sign the treaty or resume fighting. The new German government sent representatives by train to Germany to sign without negotiations. The Germans ultimately had no say in the peace terms.

The Treaty of Versailles was signed on June 28, 1919, in the Hall of Mirrors in the Palace of Versailles. Delegates streamed into the palace, and newspaper correspondents and throngs of spectators hovered outside. Everyone wanted to catch a glimpse of this momentous historic event. For two figures in particular, however, it was a dark day. The German foreign minister Hermann Müller and Johannes Bell, who was the colonial secretary of a Germany that had been stripped of its colonies, represented Germany at the ceremony.

After the war with France in 1871, the Germans had chosen the Hall of Mirrors to announce the founding of the German Empire. Now, Müller and Bell signed a treaty that symbolized defeat for Germany in the same symbolic place. "This is a great day for France,"[65] remarked Georges Clemenceau, who presided over the signing. In Germany, however, it was a day of mourning. The overwhelming feeling in Germany was that the treaty was unfair. People felt the terms of the treaty would ruin Germany. Above all, it injured German pride, just as French pride was wounded after France's defeat in 1871.

## Disappointment with the Treaty

The Treaty of Versailles created the League of Nations, which came into being after the war, just as Woodrow Wilson had hoped. Not all, however, agreed that an international body was the best way to solve the world's problems. Chief among the critics was the U.S. Congress, which refused to ratify the Treaty of Versailles and refused to join the League of Nations. Wilson had failed to convince his own countrymen of his dream for a better world. The League limped on until World War II, but never managed to solve international disputes as it was intended.

Disappointment with the treaty was not limited to Germany and the United States. The British felt that the treaty was unfair to Germany, especially the harsh war reparations that were determined after the treaty was signed. In the coming years, the Germans would start to ignore the restrictions placed on their military and condemn the treaty outright. "Between the retreat of America and the treacheries of Europe the Treaties of Peace were never given a fair trial,"[66] David Lloyd George wrote.

*The soldiers who fought in World War I were the first to fight in the kind of modern, global war soldiers from around the world still engage in today.*

## Global Conflict Continues

World War I was thought to be the "war to end all wars." However, all it did was create new conflicts. Even the peace treaty that was written to end the war created tension between nations. In Germany, the high reparations crippled the economy, and the loss in the war had deeply injured German pride. These factors contributed to the desperation and anger that gave rise to the Nazi Party and Adolf Hitler's reign of terror, which began less than two decades after World War I ended.

In many ways, the fallout from World War I led to World War II. It also led to the instability that has made life difficult in many parts of Europe for nearly a century. As empires fell apart, the lands they once controlled struggled to develop their own identity and often became prey for stronger nations. Also, the division of the lands of the Middle East after World War I created resentment and conflict that can still be felt in the region today.

Because of the creation of global alliances such as the League of Nations and the United Nations, many of the conflicts fought around the world today become global conflicts. The world has grown smaller over time, and nations band together to respond to an attack on one of their allies or to respond to a common threat. World War I started a new age of warfare—one defined by international participation rather than isolationism. It also featured new weapons for fighting in this new kind of war, including tanks and airplanes. As such, it is easy to see why many people consider World War I the first modern war. It forever changed the way wars are fought around the world, and its outcome played a huge role in shaping the course of modern history.

# Notes

## Introduction: A Nagging Question

1. Quoted in Patrick Glynn, *Closing Pandora's Box: Arms Races, Arms Control, and the History of the Cold War.* New York, NY: Penguin Books, 1979, p. 269.
2. Quoted in "World War One: 10 Interpretations of Who Started WW1," BBC News, February 12, 2014. www.bbc.com/news/magazine-26048324.
3. Quoted in Philip Magnus, *King Edward VII.* New York, NY: Penguin Books, 1979, p. 269.
4. Quoted in Magnus, *King Edward VII,* p. 513.
5. Winston S. Churchill, *The World Crisis.* New York, NY: Scribner's, 1931, p. 6.
6. Quoted in Brian Gardner, ed., *Up the Line to Death: The War Poets, 1914–1918.* London, UK: Methuen, 1964, p. 127.

## Chapter One: War on the Western Front

7. Quoted in Barbara W. Tuchman, *The Guns of August.* New York, NY: Ballantine Books, 1994, p. 119.
8. Quoted in Louis Raemaekers, *Raemaekers' Cartoon History of the War*, vol. 1. New York, NY: The Century Co., 1919, p. 8.
9. Quoted in Raemaekers, *Raemaekers' Cartoon History of the War.* p. 10.
10. Churchill, *The World Crisis,* p. 11.
11. Marshal Foch, *The Memoirs of Marshal Foch.* Garden City, NY: Doubleday, Doran, and Co., 1931, p. 35.
12. Foch, *The Memoirs of Marshal Foch,* p. 117.
13. Quoted in John J. Pershing, *My Experiences in the World War*, vol. 1. New York, NY: Frederick A. Stokes Company, 1931, p. 166.

## Chapter Two: Fighting at Sea and in the Sky

14. Churchill, *The World Crisis,* p. 85.
15. Quoted in James P. Stobaugh, *British History: Observations & Assessments from Early Cultures to Today, High School Level.* Green Forest, AR: New Leaf Publishing Group, 2012, p. 221.
16. Quoted in Geoffrey Parker, ed., *The Cambridge Illustrated History of Warfare.* New York, NY: Cambridge University Press, 2008, p. 283.
17. Quoted in Cyril Falls, *The Great War.* New York, NY: Putnam's Sons, 1959, p. 212.

18. Churchill, *The World Crisis*, p. 310.

## Chapter Three: New Battlefronts

19. Churchill, *The World Crisis*, p. 325.
20. Quoted in Churchill, *The World Crisis*, p. 325.
21. Quoted in "War Corresponded Ellis Ashmead-Bartlett," Commonwealth of Australia: Gallipoli and the Anzacs, October 2014. www.gallipoli.gov.au/battle-of-the-landing/ellis-ashmead-bartlett.php.
22. Quoted in Gardner, *Up the Line to Death*, p. 60.
23. Archibald P. Wavell, *The Palestine Campaigns*. Freeport, NY: Books for Libraries, 1972, p. 21.
24. Quoted in Parker, *The Cambridge Illustrated History of Warfare*, p. 276.
25. Quoted in Byron Farwell, *Armies of the Raj: From the Great Indian Mutiny to Independence, 1858–1947*. New York, NY: Norton, 1991, p. 261.
26. Wavell, *The Palestine Campaigns*, p. 15.
27. Wavell, T*he Palestine Campaigns*, p. 14.
28. T. E. Lawrence, *Seven Pillars of Wisdom*. Garden City, NY: International Collectors Library, 1938, p. 64.
29. Lawrence, *Seven Pillars of Wisdom*, p. 74.
30. Lawrence, *Seven Pillars of Wisdom*, p. 186.
31. Lawrence, *Seven Pillars of Wisdom*, p. 165.
32. Lawrence, *Seven Pillars of Wisdom*, p. 277.
33. Wavell, *The Palestine Campaigns*, p. 167.

## Chapter Four: The Eastern Front

34. Quoted in Parker, *The Cambridge Illustrated History of Warfare*, p. 274.
35. Falls, *The Great War*, p. 220.
36. John Reed, *Ten Days That Shook the World*. New York, NY: Random House, 1960, p. 8.
37. Reed, *Ten Days That Shook the World*, p. 10.
38. Quoted in Reed, *Ten Days That Shook the World*, p. 26.
39. David Robin Watson, *Georges Clemenceau: A Political Biography*. New York, NY: David McKay, 1974, p. 298.

## Chapter Five: America Joins the Fight

40. Quoted in John Keegan, *The First World War*. New York, NY: Knopf, 1999, p. 50.
41. George Washington, "Farewell Address" (speech, September 19, 1796), National Archives. www.ourdocuments.gov/doc.php?doc=15&page=transcript.
42. Quoted in Henry F. Pringle, *Theodore Roosevelt*. New York, NY: Harcourt Brace Jovanovich, 1984, p. 408.
43. Quoted in Barbara Tuchman, *The Zimmermann Telegram*. New York, NY: Macmillan, 1966, p. 176.
44. Tuchman, *The Zimmermann Telegram*, pp. 176–177.

45. Pershing, *My Experiences in the World War*, p. 102.
46. Foch, *The Memoirs of Marshal Foch*, p. 346.
47. Quoted in Byron Farwell, *Over There: The United States in the Great War, 1917–1918.* New York, NY: Norton, 1999, p. 106.
48. Quoted in Farwell, *Over There*, p. 19.
49. Foch, *The Memoirs of Marshal Foch*, p. 368.
50. Pershing, *My Experiences in the World War*, p. 162.
51. Quoted in Farwell, *Over There*, p. 228.
52. Foch, *The Memoirs of Marshal Foch*, p. 387.
53. Quoted in Watson, *Georges Clemenceau*, p. 325.

### Epilogue: "A Peace to End Peace"

54. Quoted in David Fromkin, *A Peace to End All Peace*. New York, NY: Henry Holt, 1989, p. 5.
55. Quoted in Carl Cavanagh Hodge and Cathal J. Nolan, *U.S. Presidents and Foreign Policy: From 1789 to the Present.* Santa Barbara, CA: ABC-CLIO, 2007, p. 396.
56. Quoted in Margaret MacMillan, *Paris 1919: Six Months That Changed the World.* New York, NY: Random House, 2002, p. 495.
57. Quoted in Valerie Pakenham, *Out in the Noonday Sun: Edwardians in the Tropics.* New York, NY: Random House, 1985, p. 218.
58. Quoted in MacMillan, *Paris 1919*, p. 495.
59. Quoted in John Bagot Glubb, *Britain and the Arabs: A Study of Fifty Years, 1908 to 1958.* London, UK: Hodder and Stoughton, 1959, p. 74.
60. Quoted in Malcolm Brown, *Lawrence of Arabia: The Life, the Legend.* New York, NY: Thames and Hudson, 2005, p. 145.
61. Quoted in Robert Lansing, *The Peace Negotiations: A Personal Narrative.* New York, NY: Houghton Mifflin, 1921, pp. 260–261.
62. Lansing, *The Peace Negotiations*, p. 263.
63. Quoted in André Tardieu, *The Truth About the Treaty.* Indianapolis, IN: Bobbs-Merrill, 1921, p. 184.
64. Quoted in MacMillan, *Paris 1919*, p. 192.
65. Quoted in MacMillan, *Paris 1919*, p. 476.
66. David Lloyd George, *Memoirs of the Peace Conference*, vol. 2. New Haven, CT: Yale University Press, 1939, p. 914.

# For More Information

## Books


Adams, Simon. *World War I.* New York, NY: DK Publishing, 2014.

This overview of the First World War includes photos from London's Imperial War Museum and first-person accounts of what it was like to live and fight during this war.

Atwood, Kathryn J. *Women Heroes of World War I: 16 Remarkable Resisters, Soldiers, Spies, and Medics*. Chicago, IL: Chicago Review Press, 2014

Atwood presents the exciting biographies of 16 women from around the world who contributed to the war effort in unique and heroic ways.

Brezina, Corona. *The Treaty of Versailles, 1919: A Primary Source Examination of the Treaty That Ended World War I.* New York, NY: Rosen Publishing, 2006.

Readers discover more about the end of World War I and the peace talks that followed through a careful examination of relevant primary sources.

Foden, Giles. *Mimi and Toutou's Big Adventure: The Bizarre Battle of Lake Tanganyika.* New York, NY: Alfred A. Knopf, 2005.

This humorous retelling focuses on one of the most famous clashes between Allied and German forces in Africa.

Goodman, Michael. *World War I Spies.* Mankato, MN: Creative Education and Creative Paperbacks, 2016.

This historical account of spying during World War I includes biographies of famous spies and information about the technology used to help them do their dangerous work.

Jeffrey, Gary, and Nik Spender. *Lawrence of Arabia and the Middle East and Africa.* New York, NY: Crabtree Publishing Company, 2013.

This graphic novel details some of the most incredible exploits of fighters on the Middle Eastern and African fronts in World War I.

Remarque, Erich Maria. *All Quiet on the Western Front.* New York, NY: Ballantine Books, 1982.

Remarque's classic fictional account of life in the German trenches during World War I provides some of the clearest insights into the way this war destroyed the men who fought in it.

## Websites

**BBC Schools: World War One**
www.bbc.co.uk/schools/0/ww1/
This interactive site about World War I was created by the British Broadcasting Corporation (BBC) and features videos, games, and contemporary answers to questions about the war.

**The British Library: World War One**
www.bl.uk/world-war-one
The British Library's World War I collection is filled with primary sources and articles written by historians.

**A Guide to World War I Materials**
www.loc.gov/rr/program/bib/wwi/wwi.html
The Library of Congress breaks down its large collection of materials from World War I, including posters, newspapers, and sheet music.

**1914–1918: The Great War and the Shaping of the 20th Century**
www.pbs.org/greatwar/
This detailed look at the war, provided by the Public Broadcasting Service (PBS), includes a timeline and essays written by leading historians.

**World War I**
www.history.com/topics/world-war-i
The History Channel's World War I website provides videos and articles about major moments and figures during this time period.

**World War I in Photos**
www.theatlantic.com/static/infocus/wwi/
Alan Taylor's photo series provides readers with a closer look at many aspects of World War I—from the technology of the time period to animals in the war.

**World War I Records**
www.archives.gov/research/military/ww1/
The National Archives military records collection contains documents such as draft registration cards, intelligence reports, and the Zimmermann telegram.

# Index

**A**
Africa
  Battle of Lake Tanganyika, 34
  French colonial troops, 22
  Gallipoli campaign troops, 41
  Germany in, 14
aircraft, 22, 35–38, 56
air warfare
  bombing, 35–36, 38
  Red Baron, 37
  U.S. and, 68, 76
Al Kut (Mesopotamia), 46–48, 53
Allenby, Edmund, 45, 52
Allied Powers, 7, 13, 57, 63, 80, 82–83, 86–87
  *See also* Britain; France; United States
*All Quiet on the Western Front* (Remarque), 26
All-Russian Congress of Soviets, 64
Alpini, 59
Alsace-Lorraine, 13, 18, 78
American Expeditionary Force (AEF), 70–71
American Flying Corps, 68
Anglo-Persian Oil Company, 45
Aqaba (Palestine), 52
Arab Revolt, 49–51
Argonne Forest, Battle of, 77
armistice, 7, 77–78, 80
arms race
  as cause of World War I, 10, 14
  Germany and, 27
  naval, 30
Ashmead-Bartlett, Ellis, 41
Asian colonial troops, 22
Atatürk, 45
Australia and New Zealand Army Corps (ANZACs), 41, 43
Austro-Hungarian Empire
  army, 58, 60
  assassination of Franz Ferdinand, 8–9
  decline, 58
  1914 offensive and, 56
  surrender and collapse, 79, 82, 87
  ultimatum to Serbia, 16

**B**
Balkans
  crisis, 16
  fighting, 58
  *See also* Ottoman Empire
balloons, 35
Beatty, Sir David, 31, 33–34
Belgium
  Fourteen Points and, 81
  invaded, 16–18
  Second Battle of Ypres, 22
Bell, Johannes, 89
Belleau Wood, Battle of, 73
Bethmann-Hollweg, Theobald von, 17
Bismarck, Otto von, 15
blimps, 35
Bliss, Tasker H., 86

Bolsheviks, 57, 62–64, 83
bombers, 38
bombs, 35–36, 38
Bosnia, 8
*Bouvet* (French battleship), 41
Brest-Litovsk, Treaty of, 64–65
Britain
  colonial empire, 13–14
  Middle East and, 49, 83–84
  Royal Air Force formed, 38
  Royal Navy importance, 27–28
  supplies, 31, 67
  war declared by, 16, 18
  zeppelin raids and, 36
Brusilov, Aleksey, 57–58, 60
Bülow, Karl von, 19

**C**

Canadian soldiers, 22, 67
casualties, 8, 18, 25, 41, 77, 79
Central Powers, 7, 13, 21, 26–27, 34, 38–40, 47, 53–54, 56–57, 64, 75–76, 80, 83
  *See also* Austro-Hungarian Empire; Germany (of Wilhelm); Ottoman Empire
China
  Germany in, 14
  Japan and, 86–87
  laborers from, 22
Churchill, Winston
  on American Expeditionary Force, 71
  on British declaration of war, 18
  on cause of World War I, 10–11
  Gallipoli campaign and, 40–41, 43
  on new weapons, 34–35
  on Royal Navy, 26, 28
Clemenceau, Georges
  on demilitarization of Germany, 88
  League of Nations and, 84
  on peace terms, 78
  on Treaty of Versailles, 89
  on western front, 65
colonial empires
  expansion after war, 87
  Gallipoli campaign and, 40–41
  Germany dismantled, 88–89
  League of Nations and, 84
  prewar, 12–14
  Royal Navy and, 27
  Suez Canal, 47
  Wilson and independence for, 82–83
Communists, 57, 62–63
Council of Ten, 86

**D**

Dardanelles, 41–43
Dearmer, Geoffrey, 43
democracy
  in China, 87
  Wilson and, 81
dirigibles, 35–36
dreadnoughts, 29–31

**E**

eastern front
  collapse, 63–64
  location, 12, 54
  trench warfare and, 54
East Prussia (Germany), 54, 56
Edward VII, 10
Egypt, 40–41, 47–48
Egyptian Expeditionary Force, 48–49, 52
Escadrille Américaine, 68

**F**
Faisal, 49, 84
Falkenhayn, Erich von, 52
father of the Turks, 45
February Revolution (1917), 61–63
fighter aircraft, 35–38
Foch, Ferdinand
  American troops and, 70
  on First Battle of the Marne, 19
  on race to the sea, 20
  on trench warfare, 77
  Second Battle of the Marne and, 74–75
Foden, Giles, 34
Fokker aircraft, 37
Fourteen Points, 80–81, 83–84, 87
France
  aircraft, 36–38
  Battle of Verdun and, 23, 25–26
  colonial empire, 13–14
  defense of, 18
  Fourteen Points and, 82–85, 88
  Middle East and, 83
  relations with Germany, 9, 12–13
  supplies, 31
  war declared on, 16
Franz Ferdinand (archduke of Austro-Hungarian Empire), 8, 10
French, Sir John, 18, 22
Freyberg, Bernard Cyril, 42

**G**
Galicia, 55–56
Gallipoli campaign, 40–49, 53
George, David Lloyd, 84, 88, 90
George V (king of England), 83
Germany (of Wilhelm)
  aircraft, 35–38
  blamed for World War I, 10–11
  blockade of, 31
  colonial empires and, 13–14
  declaration of war on France, 16
  High Seas Fleet, 30–31, 33–34, 41, 77
  Lenin and, 57, 62–64
  navy buildup, 14, 27, 29–30
  sinking of *Lusitania* and, 32–33, 67
  *See also* Wilhelm II (kaiser of Germany)
Germany (republic)
  armistice, 77–78
  Paris Peace Conference and, 80
  Treaty of Versailles, 88–89
Grand Fleet, 30, 33–34
Grey, Sir Edward, 10, 30

**H**
Hague Conference, 22
Haig, Douglas, 73
Hamilton, Sir Ian, 41
Handley Page bombers, 38
Harlem Hellfighters, 72
Hashemite kingdoms, 84
Heligoland Bight, 31
Herzegovina, 8
High Seas Fleet, 30–31, 33–34, 41, 77
  *See also* naval warfare
Hindenburg, Paul von, 55
Hipper, Franz von, 33, 34, 77
HMS *Aboukir*, 31
HMS *Cressy*, 31
HMS *Dreadnought*, 29
HMS *Hogue*, 31
HMS *Indefatigable*, 34
HMS *Irresistible*, 41
HMS *Lion*, 34
HMS *Ocean*, 41
HMS *Queen Mary*, 34
House, Edward M. (Colonel), 82

House of Hapsburg, 58
Hungary, 58, 82

**I**
Ibn Sa'ūd, 84
independence
  of Hungary, 82
  in Middle East, 82–84
  of Poland, 81
  principle of self-determination, 87
India
  Muslims, 49, 52
  Suez Canal, 52, 47
  troops from, 44, 46
*Influence of Sea Power Upon History, 1660–1783, The* (Mahan), 29
international law, 17–18
international trade, 27
Iraq, 40, 44, 52, 83–84
isolationism, 66, 70, 90
Italy
  Austro-Hungarian Empire and, 14, 58–59, 64
  reason for entry into war, 82

**J**
Japan
  China and, 86–87
  navy, 28–29
Jellicoe, Sir John, 33, 34
Jerusalem (Palestine), 52–53
Jutland, Battle of, 33–35

**K**
Kemal, Mustafa, 43, 45
Kerensky, Aleksandr, 61–64
Kitchener, Herbert, 40–41
Kluck, Alexander von, 19

**L**
Lafayette Escadrille, 68
Lake Tanganyika, Battle of, 34
Lansing, Robert, 82, 87
Lawrence, Thomas Edward, 49–52, 85
League of Nations, 84–87, 89–90
Lebanon, 83–84
Lenin, Vladimir, 57, 62–64
Lockhart, Robert Bruce, 57
Lodge, Henry Cabot, 68
Ludendorff, Erich, 32
*Lusitania*, 32–33, 67
Luxembourg, 17

**M**
machine guns, 22, 35–37, 73, 75–77
Mahan, Alfred Thomas, 29
Marne, First Battle of, 18–20
Marne, Second Battle of, 73–75
Mesopotamian campaign, 44–46
Mexico, 6, 67–70
Middle East
  boundaries, 80, 82–83, 90
  Britain and France in, 83–84
  League of Nations and, 84
  Sykes-Picot Agreement, 82–83
*Mimi*, 34
*Mimi and Toutou's Big Adventure: The Bizarre Battle of Lake Tanganyika* (Foden), 34
mines (sea), 30, 35, 41, 43
Mons, Battle of, 18
Müller, Hermann, 89
Murray, Archibald, 48, 52
Muslims, 49, 52

**N**
naval warfare
  aircraft and, 34
  Gallipoli campaign and, 40–41

Mahan and, 29
secret codes, 33
strategies, 30, 31, 35
U-boats, 31, 32, 35, 67, 70
*See also* specific battles
neutrality policy, 7, 17–18, 64, 66–68, 70
Nicholas I (czar of Russia), 60
Nicholas II (czar of Russia), 61
no-man's-land, 21

**O**
oil, 45
Okhrana, 57
Orkney Islands, 30
Ottoman Empire
collapse, 84, 87
decline, 39–40
divided after war, 82–83
Gallipoli campaign and, 40–41, 43–44
joins Central Powers, 39
Mesopotamian campaign and, 44–46
revolt against, 49
Suez Canal and, 47
surrender of, 77

**P**
Palace of Versailles, 89
Palestine, 40, 45, 47–48, 52, 83
Paris Peace Conference
American position, 80–82
colonies and, 82–83
concluded, 89
discontent in colonies, 87
French position, 88
League of Nations and, 84–85
World War II and, 88–90
Pershing, John J, 6, 70, 76–77
Pétain, Philippe, 24–25
poison gas, 22–23
Poland, 55–56, 81–82, 87
Polar Bear Expedition, 63
Princip, Gavrilo, 8

**Q**
Qingdao (China), 14, 86–87

**R**
race to the sea, 20
rats, 21
Red Baron, 37
Reed, John, 62, 63
Reilly, Sidney, 57
Remarque, Erich Maria, 26
Rennenkampf, Paul, 54–56
reparations, 88–90
Richthofen, Manfred von, 37
Roosevelt, Theodore, 66
Royal Air Force, 38
Royal Navy, 27
*See also* naval warfare
Russia
Brusilov strategy, 60
Gallipoli campaign and, 40, 43
peace, 64
revolutions, 61–63
supplies, 56, 61
war with Japan, 28–29
*See also* eastern front

**S**
Samsonov, Aleksandr, 54–56
Sanders, Liman von, 43
Sarajevo (Austro-Hungarian Empire), 8
Saudi Arabia, 84

savior of Verdun, 24–25
Scapa Flow, 30, 33
Scheer, Reinhard, 33
Schlieffen, Alfred von, 16
Schlieffen Plan
    described, 18
    eastern front and, 54–55
    overview, 16
    success of, 19
self-determination, 87
Serbia, 16, 58
Shandong Peninsula (China), 14, 86
sick man of Europe, 43, 47, 60
Somme, Battle of the, 72–73, 76
stalemate, 20, 22–23, 39, 41, 43, 71, 75–76
strategies
    Allied eastern front, 54–56
    Allied in near East, 39–41, 49
    Allied western front, 18–19
    German 1918 spring offensive, 73
    Schlieffen Plan, 16, 18–19
    German two-front, 64
    naval, 30, 31, 35
submarines. *See* U-boats
Suez Canal, 47, 52
supplies
    Britain, 31, 67
    France, 31
    Russians, 56, 61
Sykes-Picot Agreement, 83
Syria, 47, 52–53, 83–84

**T**

tanks, 8, 74–76, 90
Tannenberg, Battle of, 55–56
Thomas, Lowell, 50
*Toutou*, 34
Townshend, Sir Charles, 45–47
Trans-Jordan, 84
Treaty of Brest-Litovsk, 64–65
Treaty of Versailles, 27, 85, 87–89
trench warfare
    Americans and, 70–71
    becomes obsolete, 76
    conditions of, 20, 22
    on eastern front, 54
    extent of trenches, 21
    poison gas and, 23
Triple Alliance, 14
Triple Entente, 14
Tuchman, Barbara, 69
Turkey
    after World War I, 83–84
    Atatürk, 45
    Gallipoli campaign and, 40–41, 43–44
    Mesopotamian campaign and, 46–47
    Suez Canal and, 47–48
    *See also* Ottoman Empire

**U**

U-boats, 31–32, 35, 67–68, 70
United Nations, 90
United States
    American volunteers, 67–68, 72, 76
    army, 70–71
    causes of entry, 32, 67–68
    importance of entry, 65–67
    League of Nations and, 84–85, 89
    navy, 29, 70
    peace delegation, 79–80
    peace position, 81
    ratification of Treaty of Versailles, 89
    war declared by, 67

**V**

Verdun, Battle of, 23–26, 57, 68, 76–77
Versailles Treaty of, 27, 85, 87–89
Vichy France, 24

**W**

Washington, George, 66
Wavell, Archibald, 47, 49, 52, 79
weapons
  air, 22, 35–38, 56
  demilitarization of Germany, 88
  Krupp factory, 16, 18
  naval, 14, 31–32, 35, 67, 70
western front
  American Expeditionary Force (AEF), 70–71
  defense of Belgium, 18–19
  importance of, 65
  location, 12
  1918 spring German offensive, 73
  race to the sea, 20
  *See also* trench warfare; specific battles
White Russians, 57, 63
White War, 59
Wilhelm II (kaiser of Germany)
  ambitions of, 10
  diplomacy and, 15
Wilhelmine Germany. *See* Germany (of Wilhelm)
Wilson, Woodrow
  Colonel House and, 82
  democracy in new world order, 81
  Fourteen Points, 80–82
  League of Nations and, 84–85
  neutrality policy, 65, 66
  sinking of *Lusitania*, 32
World War II, 24, 87–90

**Y**

Ypres, Second Battle of, 22

**Z**

zeppelins, 35–36, 38
Zimmermann, Arthur, 67
Zimmermann telegram, 68–69

# Picture Credits

Cover Hulton Archive/Getty Images; pp. 6–7 (background), 11, 21, 23, 36, 38, 46, 55, 59, 61, 71, 72, 75, 78, 88 Everett Historical/Shutterstock.com; pp. 6 (top left, bottom), 7 (top left, top right, bottom), 15, 29, 30, 32, 51, 53, 67, 80, 90 courtesy of the Library of Congress; pp. 6 (top right), 57, 58 Photos.com/Thinkstock; pp. 9, 19, 74 Universal History Archive/UIG via Getty Images; pp. 13, 17 ekler/Shutterstock.com; pp. 24, 28 Ann Ronan Pictures/Print Collector/Getty Images; p. 25 Harlingue/Roger Viollet/Getty Images; p. 33 MPI/Getty Images; pp. 37, 40 Bettmann/Getty Images; p. 42 Leemage/UIG via Getty Images; pp. 44, 50, 83 Print Collector/Hulton Archive/Getty Images; p. 45 istanbul_image_video/Shutterstock.com; p. 48 Rainer Lesniewski/Shutterstock.com; p. 62 DeAgostini/Getty Images; p. 65 ullstein bild/ullstein bild via Getty Images; p. 69 courtesy of the National Archives; p. 81 JHU Sheridan Libraries/Gado/Getty Images; p. 85 Pavel Elias/Shutterstock.com; p. 86 Galerie Bilderwelt/Hulton Archive/Getty Images.

# About the Author

**Elizabeth Morgan** has worked as a writer ever since graduating from college with her degree in history. She is the author of several nonfiction books for children and young adults on a variety of topics. She lives in a suburb of Buffalo, New York, with her husband, two children, and dog named Kylo. When she is not writing, she loves spending time outdoors, reading, and traveling with her family.